Beyond Good Parenting

Beyond Good Parenting

The Art and Science of Learning, Behavior, and Partnership

by Martin L. Dutcher

Three Friendships Company 2013

First Edition

ISBN 978-0-9893205-2-8

Library of Congress Control Number: 2013949960

http://threefriendships.com

This book is dedicated to the young children of Amazing Life Games Preschool, now adults and many with their own children, with whom I had the honor and opportunity to play and learn alongside, and to their parents, who trusted us to take great care of them.

This book is also dedicated to my daughters, Brynn and Auguste, for whom I hope parenting, if chosen, is as a fulfilling and joyous, and challenging, as it has been for me as your dad.

Table of Contents

Index of Stories

Acknowledgments

I first thank Monica Aring, who first suggested that I write a book after a wonderful dinner conversation with my family at my home. Thank you, Monica, for saying just what was wanted and needed at the moment.

I thank my friend of 40 years, Josie Devine Jordan, whom I met in DC one summer. Our work together at Amazing Life Games Preschool in Washington, DC, and the lifetime friendship of our families is a joy in my life.

There are members of several organizations that opened my eyes to see things I wouldn't have seen without them. I acknowledge them here:

- The Living Stage Theater, an outreach of the Washington, DC, Arena Stage;
- Robert Alexander, its founder, and
- Rebecca Rice and Jennifer Nelson, the actors who worked with us, the preschool staff and the children at Amazing Life Games.

From these amazingly creative people I learned how to set up and play within a creative learning social environment.

Also, I thank the founders of The Institutes for the Achievement of Human Potential, a Philadelphia-based educational organization, for sharing what they have learned about the capacity and process involved in how much young children can and do learn, and how parents can facilitate that.

I thank the course leaders and trainings offered by Landmark Educational Corporation, whose staff and volunteers have contributed to my exploration of my own learning boundaries, as well as my own behavior with regard to my personal well-being and family relationships. This has been invaluable.

I thank Philip N. Adams, founder of Child's Play Learning Centers, who gave generously of his skills and commitment in service to families over the 12 years we worked together, and for his sharing his expertise in context and family dynamics.

As for the booking writing process, I especially thank fellow coursemates Dori Ackerman and Bob Herbst, and personal friend and supportive confidant, Donald Berkemeyer. I thank those who read the early versions (tough going!) but could see the potential and told me so. These include Dori Ackerman, Ina Ames, Monica Spiese, my wonderful brother-in-law, Alan Kirk, and local psychologist and family counselor, Ron Vogt. I thank the later readers, including Joseph O'Day, Clark Line, Zayba Ghazali, good friend Bill Jordan, another amazing brother-in-law, Dave Shaub (whom I also thank for honoring the intent of this book over his promise to not comment on the content), and author, friend, and parent advisor, Rick Ackerly, Ed.M. I thank Kevin Kautz for our morning conversations, which contributed to my understanding of the evolutionary, cultural and linguistic impacts on human behavior, his excellent distinctions in the definitions of words I thought I knew, (as well as ones I knew I didn't know). Thank you all for honoring my intentions as you dealt with my content and style!

The final key to a successful book-writing process is the completing-the-book process, and without the support of my publishing consultant and now friend, Teman Cooke, I might still be sitting in coffee shops writing. Thank you, Teman, for your commitment to the quality of all that you have done to bring this project to print.

I thank both my daughters, Brynn and Auguste, who have been intimately involved in my "educational exploration" of early learning, and in my activity as a parent, and as an author. They have been encouraging, inspiring, honest, and loving. Brynn, in her second and third years, attended late board meetings with me, helped me unpack our first center's classroom equipment and supplies two years later, and substituted in that very center fourteen years later. Auguste, seven years younger, was both my student and "advisor" as I designed and implemented a combined kindergarten-first grade curriculum in Reston, VA. Auguste has also contributed her perspective in several places in the text. Both have been generous. Auguste gifted me with a custom blog website, while Brynn, after two years with CityYear in Philadelphia, then teaching first grade in The Bronx, and now in a masters program in communication and design, gifted me with the cover art and design of Beyond Good Parenting. In countless ways, I am a happy father.

Lastly, I thank my beautiful friend, co-parent, and wife, Carolyn, for inspiration and support in times when I couldn't generate those myself. As a CNM, she has warmly welcomed hundreds of newborns into the world, and her studies influenced my interest and attention to the earliest stages of childhood and their importance. Her loving appreciative manner with mothers and babies always moves me. Her commitment to our family's health and well-being, and her push to keep me moving to express myself (figuratively and literally) has supported me throughout. I thank her for making this work accessible and worthwhile, and to her commitment for parents to have extraordinary lives.

Preface

I still remember the first time I actually met a young child, face-to-face. I was twenty-two, and the child was two. I was mystified. I knew nothing about young human beings. I didn't know whether I even liked them or not. But I never forgot this first experience.

It took me many years to fully appreciate the job that parents have, that every parent has, when a child is born. And I knew, at some point, if I were going to be as successful with parents as I was with young children, that I would have to appreciate any and every parent unconditionally, just like it felt natural for me to appreciate every young child I encountered (most of the time!). As a parent myself, and with my wife, Carolyn, we have "raised" two amazing young women, Brynn and Auguste, both of whom not only contributed to my working with preschoolers and school-age children, but also contributed greatly to my personal development, my work with parents, and to the writing of this book. And as much as it looks like Carolyn and I succeeded as parents on our own (don't we all parent on our own?), we had many friends and colleagues who were open, honest, respectful, appreciative, and supportive of our children and family.

I began writing Beyond Good Parenting in 2008, and its contents are a result of over 30 years of experience and independent study. Its unfolding was guided by 25 years of working and playing with young children and their families: twelve years in a classroom of three- to four-year-olds in a community preschool, four years in a classroom of five- to eight-year-olds, and another twelve years in a multi-site child care program where I directed the programs; hired, trained, and coached directors and staff; designed curricula; and subbed in the classrooms (and as needed, drove vans and unstopped toilets). In addition, I attended hundreds of hours of annual CE credits, read many books and articles on children, families, and parenting, and explored both historical and emerging ideas written by scholars and researchers in the fields of psychology, human development, neuroscience, philosophy, linguistics, sociology, anthropology, and evolutionary biology.

One of the important things I learned was this: that although the academic fields, through research and observation, have a great deal of valuable knowledge to contribute, the practice of parenting and even the practice of parent education take place in very significantly different dynamic environments. This book focuses on the experience of parenting itself, in which you, reader, are in charge, with your agenda, and your children know that. You also have enough experience to be an expert. You may not be aware of that, but you will be soon. Some things, I assert, got in the way of your using what you have learned from your own experience.

Very early in life, especially as babies, you and I were at first free to explore and experiment, looking for new experiences and ideas. But it wasn't long before we were taught to look for the right answers and the right strategies, having to set aside our innate exploratory and experimenting (learning) nature, and ignore our own personal development. We were loaded up with "shoulds" and "shouldn'ts", and we became pretty much experts at dealing with the world on those terms. But that way of approaching the world, and the thoughts, feelings, and behaviors that result from that view, as useful as they can be, also have limitations. The world of what should and shouldn't be is a very different world from the world of what is and what could be. This book is an invitation for you see the world through a different lens – a lens that enables you to see more clearly what actually is happening in your parenting, moment by moment, and through that lens there is much to be re-examined, absorbed, imagined, and accomplished. And through that lens, you will find that parenting can bring more joy, more success, and more fulfillment than you currently experience, and without giving up your own personal and professional goals.

Parenting is and always will be challenging. If it weren't, it also wouldn't be rewarding. My goal is for you to meet your specific parenting challenges successfully and in partnership with your children and parenting partners. As you learn to do this, your young child will learn with and from you – automatically – no teaching required! In the process, they will learn what it means to be responsible, and to honor themselves, you, and others. At the same time, you will discover newly what an able, loving, and powerful parent you already are.

The Skinned Knee Incident

One afternoon I was at the Lego table. I was 24 years old. I was almost always at the Lego table, surrounded by three or more three- and four-year-olds. This was my first year "teaching" at a small community preschool in Washington, D.C., after having resigned from my computer science job. As I was chatting with Rachel, a new three-year-old, I heard someone wailing and looked up. It was Richard, a young three-year-old. He came in from the backyard play area. He was crying loudly and asking, "Where's my mom!?" His mom was one of the three teachers at the small community preschool.

"She's not here now, Richard. She went to pick up some paper. What's happening?"

"I want my mom!!", he was crying and almost yelling. I could see that he was holding his knee and there was blood running down his shin.

"Well, she's not here — what happened?" I asked as I stooped down and moved closer.

"I fell down ...", he managed to say while continuing to cry. "... On the sidewalk. It hu-u-rts!!" he cried.

"I can tell," I said warmly. Then I added, "That's a good thing, that it hurts." I was surprised that I said that.

Of course that didn't help him get what he wanted, and he cried more loudly and adamantly, "I want my MOM!!!!"

I moved a little closer and sat down on the floor. "Richard, she's not here now — she'll be back in a little while ..." and added, "... I meant that it's good for it to hurt since you fell on it on the cement and broke the skin." He started to make eye contact with me but was still crying and catching his breath. After a pause, I continued. "Hurting is how our body tells us where something needs attention — like your knee right now. And you did exactly the right thing by coming in to get help." He was listening.

"Come here and let's take care of it!" I said with as much eye contact as I could get. He came over to me. "Let's take a look ...".

"It's BLEEDING!!!" he suddenly cried louder, after seeing the blood.

"Yes, it IS!" I said, and added emphatically, "And that's good, too!" He was looking at me, and still crying but I did have his attention. "Richard, your knee is working perfectly right now, and I can tell it really hurts. Hurting is how your knee makes sure that you take care of it right away, and bleeding is how it begins to take care of itself. Having some blood run out keeps bad things from going in. It keeps it

cleaner. And that's why I said 'Good!' when you told me it was bleeding."

This was a new experience for the both of us. Perhaps he had never had someone treat him like he was fine and nothing was wrong while he was having pain. And likely he was afraid that something was wrong. My talking with him relieved not only his fear but helped him understand how well his body was working – his knee was asking for attention, telling him to get help. He began to understand that everything was not only okay, but going quite well despite the pain, despite the blood, and despite that his mom was not around at the moment. Everything about him was actually working normally and perfectly, and he didn't know that. He had reacted as if pain and bleeding means something is very wrong, causing him additional fear and anxiety. Looking through a new lens, he relaxed, and his pain lessened as he began to consider that everything was working normally – that nothing was wrong, including his crying and his looking for his mom. And I had never tried speaking and acting like that … I didn't want to seem uncaring and cold. Aren't our typical responses more like concern and attempt to comfort as if we also think something is wrong? Not that there is anything wrong about that response – that was my initial reflex, but I noticed that, in responding with a reassuring tone along with relevant information, my caring about and for Richard was very real in a new way.

My last statement to him was, "Richard, great job. You did everything just like you should have." This whole event only took a few minutes, and when his mom found out what happened, she was amazed that he was over it so fast.

The "skinned knee day" marked the beginning of my realization that we so often act as if we really don't know much about children, about what they can handle, what they know, how they learn, and what is possible. Little did I know that from that moment on, that my life would become about learning and playing with children in preschools, childcare centers, and interacting with their parents.

Over the next few years I began looking for the answers to several questions, starting with these:

Why aren't all of our children excelling in our schools? Why do our children frequently continue to behave in ways that frustrate us, even though (I have discovered and soon you will too) they really want us to be happy? Why aren't we learning and educating our own children on how human behavior works rather than focusing on getting them to be nice, and to do all the things we think they should, and why then are we resorting to forms of coercion, like threats and bribery, when they don't? What possible parental role could we come up with to replace our habitual but unsatisfying ones: critic, enforcer, martyr, teacher – or does good parenting require these?

This book is about my discoveries in those areas – from my years of work with children and parents, raising two children, and my ongoing study. But not to worry – this is a practical guide, and does not require knowing anything other than what is in this book, nor does it require believing in any specific educational, academic, or theological philosophy. This is all about you and your child.

> *One day, after we had finally opened our first educational child care center (and after working in a community preschool for twelve years), the president, Philip Adams, asked me, "Marty, I'll bet you don't know what it is that you do that works in your classroom."*
>
> *My first thought was, "Yes I do!" My second thought was, "No... I don't."*

That brief conversation was a challenge unbeknownst to me at the time. It seems I began working on the question years before it was asked, and most certainly afterward.

I. Setting Up Your Journey

*I*f *there is a path it is someone else's path and you are not on the adventure.*

– Joseph Campbell

Navigating our parenting today could be compared to taking a car trip. Choosing a destination determines which roads you could take to get there. What is your destination? What kind of experience do you want to have on the drive (in your parenting)? Do you want more cooperation, more joy, or no more power struggles? Maybe it would be to not have schooling issues, like how to get your child to do homework or get higher grades. Or maybe it is just eliminating the worry and concern about your children. It may be all of these and more. It is up to you.

As with a car trip, there is no point in going faster, or putting on the brakes, or turning left or right, either, until we know where we are and where we are going. If our current map is not getting us to where we want to go, there are several possible reasons why not. We may not realize where we are at the moment, or the destination may not be clear. We may be driving on old worn out roads with many detours, in which case we may need an updated map. Often in life, and especially in parenting, we start driving and just deal the best we can with the potholes and detours, never arriving at, and maybe even giving up hope that we'll ever get to the destination we had hoped for.

Consider this radical idea: what if every problematic behavior (pothole or detour) could be turned into a learning opportunity that moves you forward rather than being added to a pile of energy-sapping frustrations and concerns? Instead of thinking "maybe he'll outgrow it," or "I heard about this stage," or "I guess my (biking, eating out, sex life, etc.) is over for a while," what if you could point in the direction you want to go, find a new route, and end up where you intended – while including (biking, eating out, sex life, etc.)? Maybe what you really want could take less time and less work than you think.

As we begin this journey, I will define certain words in the text to keep us on the same page. Many of these will be words you know and use all the time. Some words may depend on the context for their meaning; others may mean something different to other people. For example, if you were to say, "I want my child to enjoy learning," I might ask what you mean by 'learning'? Do you mean being taught in school and passing tests? Do you mean building the Lego castle the way it looks on the box? If you were to say, "I am having a hard time disciplining my child," I might ask what you mean by 'discipline'? Do you mean getting your child to do what you want her to do when you want her to? Or do you mean having her choose to be supportive and responsible? I've also included my reflections on certain terms in Appendix III.

For example:

Apprehend v. To grab or take hold of

I would like for you to apprehend the distinctions and concepts in this book in the most basic sense – "to take hold of" or "to grasp". It is in the apprehension of a new idea that makes it a usable and valuable tool. Frequently, when there is no sense of unease, or some low level avoidance of the idea, it is not likely really new. Your seizing or capturing the concepts herein is critical to your understanding of them. You can "understand" how a hammer works, but it is not a useful tool until you have "taken hold of" one and hit a nail with it.

I will use the word 'learning' to describe several modes of acquisition of the following :

Experiential knowledge[1]**:** Children explore objects using all of their senses. They learn how heavy a baseball is, how soft a cat is, how long an inch is, and what cat food tastes like (one of ours did!) and record this data. Over time, the senses of sight, sound, touch, taste, and smell become finer and finer. The refinement of these sensory abilities contributes to such things as "perfect pitch," the ability to estimate size, weight, and strength (breaking point) of materials accurately, and how things work. This kind of learning begins at birth. Experiential knowledge is acquired very fast. It happens effortlessly and naturally for a healthy and normal human brain (except under stress, fear, or potential threat).

Conceptual knowledge: This is knowledge and use of ideas and representations. The sounds (speaking) and sights (reading) of words allow us to create and experience in new and more abstract ways. Words themselves are representational: the word "cat" is obviously not a cat itself. It represents the listener's experience of "cat" just as does a picture of a cat. Both the word and a picture of a cat create an experience of a cat consisting of past associations with other experiential data (the feel of the fur, the sharpness of the claws, etc.). Layers of knowledge grow out of experiential learning and then out of increasingly complex and abstract concepts. For example, the concept of

---

1   This is also known as "concrete knowledge."

acceleration is based upon the understanding of velocity (speed). And velocity cannot be understood without the experience of distance and time. A baby begins to learn about distance and time (as well as many other things) as soon as she begins reaching for objects and moving herself forward or backward.

Memorization: When we memorize information, we intentionally "store"[2] specific information into memory for recall later. Our memory automatically grows with repetitious and/or with highly rewarding or highly threatening experiences. While we adults may associate memorization with testing, young children often display extremely accurate memory long before they get to school. Many kinds of memories are recalled over and over without our being conscious of them. That leads to the next kind of learning.

Skill-building: This type of learning involves repetitious physical behavior and includes communication. It occurs through trial and error, and then more trial and error. Mastery requires trial and error. We might call this practice, but I am avoiding that term at the moment.[3] Learning to walk, snap Legos together, or play cooperatively, these happen with when a desire and an opportunity to practice (intrinsic choice, i.e., play) are present. And every skill is acquired in small steps. For example, exposure to and opportunities for scribbling build both pre-drawing and pre-writing skills by developing, neurologically, large-to-small motor control as well as eye-hand coordination. The rate of acquiring any skill is determined by the amount of practice, opportunity, and support, and by how little fear of failure and

---

2   I use the word "store" here because that is what most of us have learned, but later we'll see that memory is much more of a process than merely getting some "thing" from the closet.

3   Many of us have had "practice" imposed upon us (extrinsically, typically by a parent or teacher). That associated experience is very different from trial and error.

pressure are present. I will sometimes refer to skills as compet-encies. I include social skills in this kind of learning.

Failing, by the way, is finally beginning to be seen as a huge oppor-tunity for learning. This happens more in the business/entrepren-eurial domain, ironically (or tragically), than in the educational domain. When we fail at something, we have the opportunity to self-correct as well as opportunities to experience the value of per-sistence, collaboration, teamwork, and coaching. Trying something else and asking for support is valuable. For reasons we will discuss later, when parents or teachers punish[4] children for failure, it is det-ental to the natural learning process, yet painful or upsetting ` environmental consequences of failure, such as falling ᴉe sidewalk, rarely have this same 'set-back' effect. No ᴇs the sidewalk was punishing them, will punish them, or ᵖting to change their behavior. But young children learn to e intent of adults very early.

npetencies are not developed merely from the gathering, under-anding, or analysis of knowledge, but from practicing. Walking, piano-playing, even noticing what we are thinking or feeling is a competency. By the way, being a parent also gives you many oppor-tunities to experiment and practice your own communication skills. I hope you will practice what you learn in this book. If you are will-ing to be actively engaged in the practice, stumbling and sometimes failing as you go, asking questions of the people around you, and getting feedback on how you are doing, the journey will be well worth your time and energy.

Final notes and thoughts: Though I frequently use a specific gender pronoun in a discussion, unless otherwise stated, every discussion applies to boys and girls, moms and dads, and men and women.

---

4   This includes embarrassing, berating, insulting, threatening, isolating, and can even include lowering, or giving a lower, grade, especially if the child's parents are upset at their child for it.

Also, you will find this book written in a more conversational tone than a textbook or training manual. I developed the concepts and distinctions from my work with preschoolers, preschool staff, parents, and with my own children, Brynn and Auguste (both of whom have made significant and essential contributions in both my thinking, learning, and writing). I began putting these ideas together in a series of parenting workshops more as a discovery process for parents rather than a teaching or knowledge-based course. I recommend you approach this book as such, thinking about what is being said, and seeing if you see what I am suggesting in your own life, both as a parent and as you recall your own growing up. It doesn't matter if you agree or disagree with any of it. It matters that you engage with it as if it could work, as if it contains a key for resolving any behavioral issue that you are struggling with or concerned about in your family.

As you consider each question or proposition, and try it out, and talk about it, you will find that taking this journey yields results for all family members:

- Arguing decreases and cooperation increases.
- Tantrums and power struggles disappear.
- Appreciation becomes felt and expressed.
- Desire for and time for fun and family projects increases.
- Concerns about peers, day care, the terrible twos, and teens morph into adventures.
- Upsets are seen as normal, temporary interruptions rather than persistent problems.
- Intimacy and respect between you and your spouse/partner is restored or enhanced.
- Guilt loses its grip and even evaporates.

If this is a destination that appeals to you, then let's get started.

From Where to Where?

In the next three sections I am going to ask you to make three lists. These lists will play a big part in your learning process. I suggest that you make your lists on three separate half-sheets of paper and keeping them inserted in this book as you read it (or get a small notebook and keep it nearby). And this is a good place to stop and get three sheets of paper and a pen or pencil.

What Do You Really Want?

Despite my years working with children and parents, I was surprised when I realized that I had never really asked myself what I wanted as a parent. Many parents in my workshops also had never really asked themselves this question, or they had asked it and responded with answers like, "I want my kids to be good," or "...be happy," or "...be successful," or more short-term responses such as "I want my kids to do their homework." These are fine goals, but they don't really address the process that must occur for these goals to be met, nor do they specifically address your life, your happiness, and you getting your own "homework" done, your own goals accomplished. You are the key to the unfolding of all of it. So let's focus on you for a bit.

If anything were possible, what would you want your parenting experience to be like? What would you want to accomplish as a parent? What kind of a world would you want to live in every day? What kind of human beings do you want to be around every day? If your answer is about what your child does or doesn't do, reword it so that it is how he or she is. For example, if you are thinking, "I want him to have a clean room," that is great. Now ask yourself, what larger quality or character trait would cover that? A possible re-wording would be that he is "someone who takes good care of his environment," or "enjoys organizing and setting things up esthetically." Your answers will be clearer and more useful for you if they are also not in the negative. Here is an example: I want my son or daughter "to not give up on him/herself," which though a good start, could be worded as "be persistent with regard to his/her goals." Now, with that in mind, begin by answering the following question:

Looking 25 years ahead, what would you like to see in your child that would make you really proud of the job you have done as a parent?

On one of your sheets of paper, write "List A: What I Want" at the top. Then begin to write down what you first think of. Keeping asking the question over and over like this: "What else would I like to see?"

When you have taken enough time to make a list of ten to twenty items, take a look at Appendix I, and see if there is anything on List A, compiled from other parents, that you would like to add to your list. If you end up with over ten, that's great. Keep the whole list and underline your top three. As I ask you to refer to your List A (your "A List"), be sure and note at least your top three.

How Is It Going Now?

This exercise is about the starting point for your journey. We come from different parents, different philosophies, different social and economic circumstances, and there are many factors that influence our children's behavior and our own behavior. And within our family, our behavior and our child's behavior are entangled. But what we parents (and children) all have in common are times of success, and times of frustration, and out of some expectation we may have a general feeling or assessment ourselves as parents. As with most parents, your parenting experience probably varies from satisfying highs to discouraging lows. At times we might say, "I'm doing well … my child is good, and I am a good parent." Or we might say, "This is not what I expected … I didn't know it would be this demanding and difficult." We go from "Wow ... I am just loving this!" to "I think I made a mistake ... I'm not cut out to be a parent!" And what we say may vary, depending on the day, the time of day, or the person we are talking with.

Let's lay aside our assessments and now address specific instances of problematic behavior (aka, misbehavior). Don't write them down now or worry about remembering them. Just think about them:

- What behavior(s) in your family are you dealing with, struggling with, or putting up with? Notice when you have said or say to yourself, "oh, it's like that for every parent," or, "it could be worse," or, "at least it's not as bad as it is for so-and-so," or, "I hope she will grow out of it"?
- What do you wish were not happening?
- What do you wish were happening? (Think of times like bedtime, dinner time, getting out the door to work, dropping your child off at child care or preschool, etc.)

Here are a few examples to get you thinking and a suggested way to start each one:

My child would always:

- Eat the food I prepare for meals, and/or eat healthy food
- Appreciate me instead of demanding more
- Go to bed at bedtime (and stay there)

My child would never:

- Whine or complain
- Have tantrums
- Taunt her siblings

If I were truly being a great parent, I would never:

- Yell at my child
- Use bribery or scare tactics
- Give in to tantrums
- Blame my partner/spouse

I would always:

- Know the right thing to say
- Give my child my full attention when we are talking
- Always serve healthy food

At the top of another one of your sheets of paper, write "List B: What Should or Shouldn't Be Happening." Here is the question to ask yourself, and now write down your answers:

If I were really doing a great job as a parent, what should or shouldn't be happening? What should or shouldn't my child be doing? What should or shouldn't I be doing or saying?

When you have finished List B, read the list created by other parents in Appendix I, List B. If there's anything you see there that is also true for you, add it to your list now.

Before you put it aside, take a close look at your List B. Notice that the items you have listed actually define your current underlying notion of what it means to be a "really great parent." If you were really a great parent, wouldn't all those things be handled? But we all know that is not possible, don't we?

Now, ask yourself this: Who said your kids, or you, should or should not do this or that, or say things like that, or act a certain way? Who made this up? If you think you did, when did you do that (how long ago, and how much time did you spend on it)?

It is useful for you to recognize that you didn't originate this list. I didn't deliberately and thoughtfully choose every item on my list either, and neither did our parents. We didn't sit down with either our parents or our parenting partners one day and say, "Hey, let's make up a list of how parenting should go, okay?" No, we adopted our list — automatically and unconsciously — when we were very, very young. And now we feel and act as though the list is not merely ours, but it is "the truth" about the way parenting should or shouldn't go. Is it possible that how you and I feel about our parenting, especially at times of stress, is being determined by our inadvertent adoption of that list? (Note: it is not that we consciously think that our list is the truth — we are smart, we know better. But notice that we frequently feel, talk, and act as if it were. There are several reasons why we do this, which we will cover in chapters 3 and 4.)

Take a look at your list again. Now see if you can tell where your adopted ideas came from. Here are some possibilities:

- Your own upbringing — that is, things you learned that you should and should not do from your parents
- What your pediatrician told you
- What you have heard or read
- What your parents or other adults have criticized you for
- What you (silently or with others) criticize other parents for or gossip about

What to take from this exercise going forward is an awareness of the pre-existing expectations we already have, that we started parenting with, and that our sense of how our parenting is going comes not from what is happening (specific behaviors), but what we think should or shouldn't be happening (aka, misbehaviors). And if you haven't already thought of this, every parent likely has a somewhat different set of expectations. This is also the source of arguments and strife between you and your parenting partner, and/or you and your parents about parenting.

Finally, consider this: your List B, instead of being something to feel bad about or to attempt to eliminate, could actually be the hidden directions to your "List A: What I'd Like to See in My Child 25 Years From Now". Consider that List B is your syllabus. Each "should" or "shouldn't" on your list is, itself, an opportunity for you and your child to learn a new cooperative competency – the results of which will show up in action, in behavior, and in partnership. Consider that if you or your child never got upset or "mis"-behaved, it would take all of the learning and all of the challenge out of parenting and thus, all the satisfaction and rewards as well. I am not kidding!

Of the two lists you have – courageously – made thus far, notice this: List A is about the future. List B is about the past's interpreta-tion (meaning) of the present. So we are going to travel from List B to List A as a way of life, as a way of parenting (as a competency), with opportunities every day. The items on your List B are the road signs that lead to your List A – as you will see as we go along.

Your Hidden Parenting Manual

I know you've heard that children don't come with a "how to par-ent" manual, but they do. Actually, you and I received (learned) most of it as we were growing up, although we may have added a few things to it since then. This manual has the strategies to use, and how to do this and how to do that, and what you and your child should and shouldn't do, and how to tell if you are a good or bad parent. In some circumstances, it is pretty darn useful. But it also has an agenda that may be at odds with what you want. That is why you made your List A. List A, not this inherited manual, is your compass. Now let's look at what instructions are in the manual you are currently using.

These already existing instructions are the strategies that you are currently using. What strategies do you use to get your child to do what you want him or her to do? You do have them, and more than one. You will try one ("Jimmy, go clean your room"). And if/when that one doesn't work, you may try another one ("Now!"). And if/when that doesn't work you try another one ("One. Two....") And if/when that one doesn't work, you're on to the next one, or, if you're out of them, maybe you look for a parenting class or just begin to "bear it."

We parents are really all in the same boat, using the same manual (but perhaps each with our own footnotes). There won't be any strategy on your list that every parent hasn't used, myself included, either intentionally or unintentionally, or at least considered in a moment of frustration.

It might help to go back to the last specific times your child did not cooperate or did something you wanted her or him to correct. For example, imagine it is bedtime. Your young child is not cooperating. In fact, she seems to be thinking of everything that could thwart or delay the process: "I'm hungry", "I'm thirsty", "I want my other bear", "I forgot to say goodnight to Alvin", "catch me if you can..." What do you do? What do you say? How do you act? Each act is a strategy or is a part of a larger strategy. This is your own list, so you can be completely authentic here. Do you threaten them? Bribe them? Get angry? Just let loose? Whatever strategy you have used, know that probably every other parent reading this book has used it too. Think about how long parenting has been around. What is left to try?

On a third sheet of paper, title your list "List C: My Strategies." Below is the question for you to answer. Be as descriptive as you can: what do you say; how do you say it; how do you act; etc.

***What do you do in order to get your child to do what you
want them to do, when you want them to do it, and they
refuse, delay, or ignore you?***

Write each strategy down. After you write one down, don't stop.
Look for another strategy you use, or one your parents used or your
partner uses. If a particular strategy doesn't work, then what do you
try next? And if that doesn't work? Write down each of these
strategies. Keep going until you've got a list of ten to twelve things
you've tried to get your child to do what you want, whether they
were successful or not.

Good! You just wrote out your hidden parenting manual. But it is
not just yours. Every parent and early childhood teacher has this
same list. And when one doesn't work, we move on to the next one.
Where did this manual come from?

A few years ago I led a course for young people (ages 10-12) called
"How to Get What You Really Want from Your Parents." It was
totally fun and amazing. They made a List C – what they do now to
get what they want. Guess what? It was almost exactly the same list
parents make in every workshop I lead! But there were two differences. At the top of their list was "act cute." (This one they learned
from observing someone in their family, yes?) And it probably is
not on your list. (Should it be?) And the next one the children listed
was "make them [parents] feel guilty." This is on your list, but not
likely at the top. It made me realize something that I think is universal: you and I, particularly as parents, won't think of the "worst"
thing we do first, and definitely we would not put it at the top of
our list, even if it is the first one we try every time. It is part of our
wanting to look good as a parent, especially to ourselves and to our
adult parent (peer) group. I used to think peer groups were only a
concern for children!

Now read through the list in Appendix I, List C. Add any strategies
from the Appendix that you also use; I want you to have them all

written down. I am not suggesting that you stop using your manual – it is all you've got at the moment. The first goal is to become aware of using it, and notice when and which strategy you are using as you use them. As we move forward, we are going to create new ways of accomplishing a partnership – that is, design a new way to interact with our children that leads to our List A – our desires.

Consider that your lists A, B, and C are your directions for moving ahead. Keep them handy (I suggest you tape them into this book).

Your List A is how we know which direction we want to go. List B includes the things that we get upset about when they happen. They are the potholes, the detours, the construction along the road. They result in feelings and thoughts about what should or shouldn't be. They reveal our beliefs and ideals about parenting, and however impractical or upsetting, their impact on us is not going to disappear all at once.

We also know that if we keep doing what is on our List C we will keep getting the same results, and keep having the same concerns. This is because our strategies, as strategies to get our children to do what we want or what we think they should, activate a universal yet never discussed "law" of human behavior. Here is what I am talking about:

The Parents' Dilemma

There is a powerful principle that I first encountered while working with Philip Adams, President and Founder of Parent University and Child's Play Learning Centers, Inc., in Reston, Virginia. We trained parents and staff in this principle, and I have not found it discussed in any of the parenting literature nor in any early childhood training, yet you will immediately feel the truth of it.

The Discipline Dilemma
by Auguste Dutcher

Next time you have the opportunity, try this exercise: Stand palm-to-palm with one of your children (or anyone else!). Begin to apply pressure to their hands. What happens? They likely push back — almost all people do. It doesn't take much to see that even a little force causes almost immediate resistance.

Let's consider all of this in regards to the parenting strategies you wrote down in your List C — the means by which you try to get your child to do what you want, when you want. Naturally, these strategies are only in place to deal with things that your child will not do of his or her own volition; otherwise, there would be no need to coerce, convince, or push them to do it. Rewards, sweet-talk, scare tactics, physical intervention, and other strategies are all ways of getting your child to do something. They are all means of force, even if they don't seem like it.

Given this observation, it is no wonder that parents face resistance; it is no wonder that these strategies do not always work on "us kids." And it's a blessing that we don't give in at the drop of a hat. Do you really want your children to learn to be immediately and unquestioningly complicit with what older, authority figures want from them?

Luckily for everyone, there is an alternative to force that works towards having what all parents want for their families, and a part of this alternative is a certain kind of communication — mostly just saying what was there all along. When my own parents talked to me about what they were doing and how they were reacting, and why they were asking something of me, force was no longer present. Without the force, there was little need to resist — moreover, I felt respected and valued as a person, simply because they were willing to talk in a straightforward way with me. Of course, there is more to great parenting than this one distinction. But again, the first step is simply to recognize your current strategies for what they are: [a kind of] force.

Did you try the exercise Auguste suggested? If not, find someone near you and ask them to do it with you. Though it appears obvious, actually doing it with someone else will help you begin to notice when this phenomenon is occurring.

Consider this: when your child resists your attempts to get him to do or to stop doing something, it means that you have a healthy child. It is a human and natural thing to do. You might notice that is not only healthy, it is actually desirable – it almost certainly leads to at least one result in your List A. Can you find one?

If force causes resistance, and punishment, rewards, bribery – all of List C – are a kind of force (we use them to get our children to do what we want, don't we?), how are we to get our children to do what we want them to do? Isn't that our job?

That is our dilemma. This force-causes-resistance is a new view of the behavior between parent and child, and teacher and student, and actually occurs between all human beings. Thus it requires some new thinking on your part to resolve. Each of the topics in the upcoming chapters is like a new view, and is one piece of a puzzle – it may be interesting in itself, but the whole picture isn't complete until all the pieces are put together. And each new view requires new thinking in order to be of value, in order to get to your List A. To use our driving metaphor, if you got really good at being able to accelerate but hadn't gotten good at left turns, or could make great left turns but couldn't stop the car … you get the idea.

Next, let's visit the nature of the unique and special relationship we have with our children when they are very young.

II. Meet the Big People

*T*he world wasn't yours. It belonged to the big people.

– Anne Sexton, "The Fury of Overshoes"[5]

The Big People
by Auguste Dutcher

My mom once had this idea for a museum exhibit designed specifically for adults. Every household object in it would be enlarged to a scale that mimicked our experience as young children. In her vision, the exhibit would be complete with expansive, high-ceiling rooms containing tables at eye-level, chairs too large to let you use the backrest or put your feet on the floor, and—her crowning touch for the museum bathroom—a toilet big enough to fall into.

From the days when I could (and on one occasion did) fall into the toilet, I remember the annoyance of having to use a stool at the sink. There came a time when I could finally reach the faucets, but even then droplets of water would run down my uplifted arms, leaving me with a damp shirt and dripping elbows. I went up the carpeted stairs on hands

---

5 Anne Sexton, "The Fury of Overshoes," The Collected Works of Anne Sexton, Houghton Miflin Harcourt, 1981.

*and knees, and down on the static-y seat of my pants. I would fre-
quently call to my mom and dad to save me from Toby the cat, who was
generally friendly but would lie in a doorway, waiting for me to try to
pass, and took advantage of my less-stable moments by knocking me
over for sport. If we played hide-and-seek with family friends, my sister
could drop me into the laundry hamper, where I'd peer through the
wicker slats knowing I'd never be found.*

*From a child's perspective, adults are big—that much is obvious.
Although I have a vivid memory of hiding from Toby, I can't quite
remember the time when adults were all I watched, and were my only
source of survival. But I know this time existed for me, as it does for
every young child. As we grow older, we may forget the challenge that a
staircase or marble-hard counter-top once represented. So it's no surprise
that by adulthood, we can scarcely fathom what a monumental role
grown-ups, beginning with our parents, played in our lives.*

Our thoughts and ideas about what it was like to be a young child,
even when we draw upon specific memories, have faded and then
been replaced. We see everything through an adult lens, through all
the ideas, understandings, and interpretations we've learned. We are
divorced from those early memories and experiences, even though
they impact us today.[6] Auguste's memory of her mom's idea for a
museum suggests a way we could begin to re-explore one aspect of
the life of a young child. Take a minute or two and try to imagine
being two feet tall. Put your hand out in front of you, about two
feet up from the floor. If your eyes where there, what can you see?
What can't you see? Now squat down on the floor with your eyes
two feet up. Look around. Imagine that you cannot get up! Do you
get a sense of what it is like for a very young child?

Another aspect of the earliest years of life is that young children are
all about growing and learning – they just do it automatically. Here
is a way to think about this kind of learning:

---

6   How and why this happens will be covered in Chapter IV.

Born to Trust

How did you learn to ride a bicycle? Wasn't it a trial and error – fail and self-correct – process? If you had someone help you by continuing to hold you in balance, you wouldn't be able to learn to balance yourself, would you? Your parent had to let you go for you to learn to balance yourself. Likely he or she just kept you from falling and hurting yourself, but let you go off balance. They provided a safe way to learn. And for a well-meaning parent to keep saying, "Keep your balance! Keep your balance!" – that really doesn't help, does it? And after you learned how to ride a bicycle, did you then have to try to keep your balance? Not really – you just did it. You were born to learn, and your parent was trustworthy – in your early view.

Just Stand Up

When Brynn, my first daughter, was about three and walking confidently, we would play simple gymnastics. I would lie on my back with my knees up. She would sit on my knees, facing me. She would put her feet in the palms of my hands, as if she were going to stand up on my hands while my elbows were on the floor by my sides. Then I would say, "Hey, Brynn, try to stand up on my hands. I am strong enough to hold you, and I can catch you if you start to fall." Brynn attempted to stand up, but her uncertainty made her feet move back and forth and I couldn't hold them steady. I could see that she was "trying" to keep her balance, and it was taking a lot of effort. So then I said, "Brynn, just stand up." She trusted me, and she stood up. It was kind of magical for both us, as she just stood there, her feet in my hands, confidently, without shaking but with small movements that did keep her in balance. Then I said, "Keep standing up," and I slowly straightened my arms, extending hands upwards, and up she went. There she was, up in the air, standing on my hands with nothing to hold onto, as my arms

*were extended upwards. She smiled, I smiled. And we loved to show off
to everybody.*

Brynn trusted my saying, "just stand up," because of a very unique
relationship between parents and children in the very early years
(and partly because of the way a part of our brain functions with
regard to that relationship).

I recommend getting a copy of Anne Sexton's poem, "The Fury of
Overshoes," from which I took the opening quote for this chapter.
Find a quiet time and place and read it. This poem expresses how
our current thinking about our early years is very different from
what our life was like for us when we were in those early years,
especially the role of adults.

Whether you are currently the parent of a young child or ever have
been, you are one of the "big people" referred to in the poem. As a
new parent, you are the perfect role-model for your very young
child because you are the only (or most significant) role-model. A
newborn baby is naturally attentive to his parent, and "mimics" his
parent's reactions. One significant way our babies learn from us is
from the way they see and hear us respond to people and things
around us. All is being carefully watched and absorbed through
their senses. The good news is that our young children cannot help
but learn from us — absolutely everything, including noticing that
Big People tell little people what to do, what's right, and what
should or shouldn't happen. This early learning is an innate and
constant activity.

You don't have to devote your time to studying or creating a curriculum to have your children learn about how to be an adult: in
their view, you have already mastered that curriculum. You are the
expert in survival. You are the curriculum. That can be the bad
news too: you cannot omit anything from this natural form of

"teaching." Here are several examples of what your children learn from you very early:

- A spoken (and essentially foreign) language
- Whether what they see or hear at any moment is useful for future attention
- What is safe to do and say, and what is not
- What is necessary for gaining and keeping your love and support
- For every upset-causing behavior, there is an acceptable explanation

There are many more than these, for sure, but these are some that we don't normally appreciate or think about. Most of the ways we impact our children's lives occur without our awareness and without our being engaged in what we call teaching.

Our children, from birth if not even earlier, are absorbing[7] our attitudes about the world. They sense them from our words, our behaviors, and other nonverbal forms of communication – our body posture, our tone of voice, the loudness of our voice, the way we move our eyes, changes in the color of our skin, even the way we taste and smell at different times. These are our pre-verbal "languages," and we still are very influenced by them whether we are conscious of them or not.

Recent studies suggest that our infants are actually learning how to "read" our emotional state by looking into our eyes and associating what we are communicating physically and verbally in those moments. In addition, the human brain contains special cells called "mirror neurons": "Mirror neurons allow us to grasp the minds of

---

7   I sometimes refer to this idea as "adopting" or "mirroring." The point is, we are the model.

others not through conceptual reasoning but through direct simulation. By feeling, not by thinking."[8]

Psychologists used to think infants merely copy (mimic) mom's facial expressions, and that not much else was happening. New research says this is far from the truth. Infants spend virtually all their time "reading" their parents' (typically) faces, tones, movements, heartbeats, and emotions as well as their internal neurological-emotional circuits, and those circuits are firing in the same patterns as a close-by parent. That is the active neurological foundation for how we learn to relate to other people. Every way children learn to relate to the world around them is founded upon the earliest perceived responses and meanings given by their mothers' eyes, faces, tones, and emotions. A mother's perceptions of her own world is also her baby's world, and that can be a place of safety and comfort – a "home-base" for all new explorations and experiences – or not. Our babies not only pick up our parental reactions to people, but they also begin to intuit what to think and feel through this attentiveness or "mind-sight."[9] This then transfers into their ability to "read" and respond to other people later in life – to get into another's world and understand them, developing empathy.

Do you ever wonder what a baby is thinking when he locks his eyes onto yours? Do you ever wonder if he is really seeing you? Isn't that an amazing experience? Yet the true nature of babies' attention and intention has been overlooked until recently. Dr. Elizabeth Spelke, a professor of psychology and a pre-eminent researcher into "babyhood" at Harvard University, asked herself, "Why did it take me 30 years to start studying this? All this time I've been giving infants objects to hold, or spinning them around in a room to see how they

---

8   Rizzolatti, G, "Cells That Read Minds", NYT (online), Dec 10, 2006, by Sandra Blakeslee

9   Siegel, Daniel, <u>The Developing Mind</u>, Guilford, 1999, p 140.

navigate, when what they really wanted to do was engage with other people!" [10]

This demand for engagement and exploration with a parent is how our children learn what is important to attend to in their environment. We might say they are learning what is "useful." But they have no idea what the concept "useful" is. Since you are there – a Big People – alive, breathing, supplying everything they need, in their "view" you certainly know what is important and what isn't. Any reaction you have to something you are observing registers with them as something real, something important to "attend" to. This includes all your nonverbal (physical, attitudinal, emotional) as well as verbal responses. Babies also note things you pay no attention to, and learn to pay no attention to them as well. [11] They do this through an innate activity called "gaze monitoring." [12] They are literally monitoring your gaze. They look at what you are looking at, and noting whether and how you attend to what you see, or if you don't. A hierarchy of important information is being created in their brains for what it means to be grown up, to be an adult human being, and to belong with you, and later, to be a part of the communities in their lives. Our young children's earliest learning about the way life is, and what certain actions mean, happens in our family living environment. You and I are our children's environment in a very powerful yet relatively unnoticed way.

Children want to experience – see, feel, smell, hear and taste – the world around them right now. That is what they are hungry for: the weight, the feel, the smell, the taste, the color(s), what something can do and cannot do, and how it is put together. No talking about the world compares. No "wait 'til later" satisfies their urge. Although our "teaching talk" (about) things is a valid way (learned

10 Angier, Natalie (interviewer), "Insights From the Youngest Minds," NYT Profiles in Science, April 30, 2012.

11 Pearce, Joseph Chilton, <u>Reaching Beyond Magical Child</u> CD series, available at Touch the Future (ttfuture.org)

12 Johnson, Stephen, <u>Mind Wide Open</u>, Scribner, 2004, p 30.

in our environments) to attempt to communicate the experience of those things to our child, what our child is actually experiencing at those moments is a Big People "talking about something." This can be a distraction from their self-determined focus, from what they are already engaged in or what is next for them.

By the way, I am not saying don't talk with your young children. Do a lot of social talk. "Social" talking with someone is very different than what I call "teaching" talk. It's also very different from what researchers have called "business" talk.[13] Telling our children what things are, in the abstract, and asking them to give us back information so we know they have learned it (i.e., testing) is what I call "teaching" talk. And "business" talk consists of directives: get your shoes on, time to eat, go back to bed, etc. What I called "talking with" is the extra "social" talk – neither "business" nor "teaching" talk – that, according to at least one study, makes the difference in language development and that leads to accomplishment and success – such as making strong (and healthy) friendships, and performance in school.[14]

Dr. Risley, an author of <u>Meaningful Differences in the Everyday Experiences of American Children</u>, puts it this way: "Here's the best description for [social talking with] babies: dancing. Dancing because both partners are sustaining the dance."[15] We usually talk to each other, our friends and even strangers, for enjoyment, for a sense of being related. We make eye contact, we notice how each other feels and each of us responds. It is a dialogue – a two-way communication which includes eye-contact and body language, and not necessarily all, or any, in verbal language. This kind of talk happens to include a lot of information that we are not aware of. We get to know each other "dancing" together in social conversation.

---

13 Hart, Betsy, and Risley, Todd, <u>Meaningful Differences in the Everyday Experiences of American Children</u>, Paul H Brooks Publishing, Baltimore, 1995.
14 Christensen, Clayton, <u>Disrupting Class</u>, The McGraw-Hill Cos., 2008, p 150
15 Risley, Todd, Interview with David Boulton, www.childrenofthecode.org/interviews/risley.htm

Children love to ask us things about ourselves. "Tell me about when you were little," is a common question we get from our children. You can use "tell me about" too, to encourage more social talk: "Tell me about your day, sweetie...," rather than "What did you do today?" Just remember they also want to know about you, especially when you were growing up. All this open and personal social conversing (back and forth) is exactly the kind of talk you cannot overdo with your child from birth on. The quantity of these social conversations determines the amount of early language and literacy development that occurs, which consists of much more than simply expanding your child's vocabulary. Doing something together, making good eye-contact, using adult vocabulary (even making puns) is a vital part of this process, and takes no extra time.

If your child is not yet talking, no matter. Look in her eyes when talking with her. See how she responds with her eyes, mouth, head, hands, legs, etc. And relax and enjoy "being" with her. Then tell her what you are thinking – in words as well as with your eyes, mouth, head, and hands. How does she respond? And then you respond to her response. This is what Dr. Risley called "language dancing."

Of course you will give your child factual information. Help her learn the names of everything. But only when she wants it, when it is relevant to a question or part of the current circumstances, and when you are also enjoying it. Note that they are not aware of most of what they are learning, nor aware that they are learning, as they engage with new information and activity. That is one of two reasons why asking our child, "What did you learn today?" usually goes unanswered. The other reason we will cover in The Children's Dilemma in Chapter V.

Our Earliest Languages

As we progress in understanding our children's learning and behavior, our taking these non-verbal messages into account can give us many insights into our child's learning and behavior.

Consider that throughout life we actually use several "languages" other than our verbal language. Here is a list, roughly from the earliest observable and learned ones to the later ones:

- Touch
- Tone of voice
- Frequency and duration of eye contact
- Facial expression
- Gestures
- Body posture
- Verbal language

Using all their senses, our very young children learn our non-verbal languages sooner than they learn our verbal language, and they learn to understand our verbal language long (relatively) before they can speak it. They are not only learning the names of things and ideas, but also the meanings of certain conversations. Sometimes these meanings are either inaccurate or not useful. A child who is frequently yelled at for his unintended misbehavior may come to think he is not loved or not wanted, whether that is true or not, and may also come to the conclusion that being an adult means yelling at children (if not everyone).

Why a frown occurs, or an eyebrow is raised, may sometimes be obvious, but at times when it is not, our likelihood of deducing another's intentions correctly is low. We have been taught, inadvertently, that when a parent or teacher gets upset, it is personal, that we did something bad or wrong. This may not be the case, and we will discuss this when we examine how our brain works.

Immersion

Consider that you and I, when we were babies, were like "aliens" in a new world. Everything was totally unfamiliar. What are the ways of this new world? Of course, the best way to learn how to live and thrive in a new place is to observe those who are native to it, and imitate what they do. As a baby, you couldn't verbally talk to your parent yet as you didn't yet understand or speak their language. But you were immersed in their talking – you observed it, felt it, and began experimenting with it. All this was being absorbed in some way. Whatever a parent repeated over and over must be important, so the neural circuits were created to experience and do it and were strengthened with practice. The neural circuits that were used to experience whatever brought pleasure or threat were built and strengthened. Additional new neural associations, including behavioral responses that either avoided or attracted pleasure and threat, were also being created and reinforced. On the other hand, experiences that were ignored did not strengthen, and many circuits withered or disappeared entirely, as they do when perceived by the early brain as not needed. This is why you and I have difficulty seeing or hearing things that others can see or hear that are unfamiliar to us. Have you noticed that when someone from a foreign country tells you her name, you have to ask several times before you can actually hear it (so that you can repeat it)?

Imagine what this is like for your child – learning the language, learning how to think about things, finding out what brings security and joy, what is dangerous, what can be said and done and what cannot be said and done. She notices what always happens (objects always fall downwards), and what never happens (daddy never flies through the air, at least not in our family), and what sometimes happens and, for example, why a bird, which does fly through the air, comes to the feeder outside your window. It must be hungry. There is food there that it recognizes, and there is no better food available in the area. Even if you don't explain all the details, your child will eventually find or figure things out, generating new neural connections and circuits as she does that.

As she becomes more familiar with verbal language, she begins to notice the consistencies and discrepancies between what is said and what is done. At an early age children have no judgment about it – they know nothing – not even that people "should" do what they say they will. Our children notice whether we do or not, and when we do and when we don't. If we say one thing and do another, that is just the way it is. How is our child going to belong and survive? She will do, or attempt to do, what we model for her to do. She will act like we act. Why else would we, her Big People, be that way and do things that way and say those things? It is the way it is. She really needs us and uses us, her Big People, to learn about all this. She must be sure we stay around, that we continue to want her, that she belongs. This is not a conscious thinking process, by the way. It is in her neural wiring, passed on from generation to generation.

What is it like for our children, being around us? What are they learning about us, their parent, in particular, and how might that affect how they see the world, and where and when can they safely explore in order to learn?

In the Coffee Shop

One morning, as I began writing a chapter for my book, a young mother and her toddler came in to the coffee shop. The mom ordered her tea and a muffin to share with her daughter, whom I heard her call Maya.

Mom sat down at a small table, and Maya stood next to her Mom's legs, leaning on them. Mom smiled down at her, and offered her a bite of the muffin. As Maya's eyes looked around, her body began to turn towards the chairs, tables, walls, artwork. She then began to walk away from Mom towards a nearby empty table, about four feet away. Mom watched, but didn't say or do anything, and every few seconds Maya looked back at Mom. Mom just calmly looked back. Then the door to the coffee shop opened, and as a customer came in, Maya quickly returned to Mom's legs, hugging them. After the door closed and the new customer had passed by, Maya looked around again. This time she toddled a little further away, over to the display case, which had some cold drinks, sandwiches, and pastries behind the glass. She was about ten feet away from her mom. Again, the front door opened, and several new customers, already engaged in a conversation, entered. Maya's attention quickly and briefly went to the entering customers, and then she returned to Mom. Again Mom just looked at her and smiled. After another minute or two, Maya restarted her exploring, and this time went a little further away from Mom. She walked around one table and came near to where I was sitting, and looked at what I was doing. I looked up, smiled, and said, "hello." She looked a bit uncertain, and turned and went back to Mom.

At one point Maya walked up to the entrance door to the street, which opened inward. As soon as she got close to the door, Mom did two things. She began to get up from her chair and go to Maya, and she gently but firmly said, "Maya, come back here away from the door." Maya did as Mom asked. Maya had enough freedom to explore and had already likely learned, through experience, there was a good reason Mom asked her to come back, and/or that there was no good reason not to do as Mom asked.

Several months later, in the same coffee shop, another young mom came in with her toddler. Initially I was reminded of Maya, but when this toddler walked away from her mom, her mom said, in a loud and harsh voice, "Get back over here! Don't you go wandering off!" The toddler did not go back to her mom, and looked like she didn't know what to do. Her mom got up, grabbed her arm and pulled the toddler next to her, not saying anything. The little girl began to cry. Her mom said, "Now stop that crying! You don't need to be crying now!" And the tod-

dler got more upset. Both her drive to explore and her need for mom's love and support were being thwarted. What solution did she have? She could find no option that would work even a little bit. Not only was there no opportunity to explore (i.e., learn), but no dependable way to get her mother's love, belonging, and support. And her mom's responses were loaded with messages about life, other people, and the toddler's self-worth and ability.

I've been talking with parents of all kinds long enough to assert that both these parents absolutely love their little girls unconditionally. From my observation, I'd say both parents were wanting to do "good parenting" at the time. Interestingly, as I did end up talking to both moms, I learned both were questioning whether they had done the right thing. I briefly told the first mom that I just loved the way she let her toddler explore and welcomed her back for a hug at any time. She said, "Oh! I was worried that I shouldn't let her walk around … I just do the best I can." The mom from a few months later had looked up and saw me watching her as she was struggling with her crying toddler and said, apologetically and with frustration, "I just don't know what to do with her … I'm sorry she disturbed you." I did my best to reassure her that I was used to being around young children, and her child didn't disturb me. Her child was not making any eye contact with anyone.

It is notable that neither parent knew what messages they were giving their little ones. They were focused on, "Am I doing this right? Am I doing a good job?" Where did this habitual concern come from, and how many years do we spend in environments that continuously imply that there is already a right answer and a good way to do everything, and thus a wrong or bad way as well? No matter our parenting style, background, or philosophy, we are all in this same parenting boat, so to speak.

Being completely open to everything – when they are safe and secure – makes learning easy for very young children. They don't yet have to know whether anything is right or wrong, or good or bad, or whether anything should or shouldn't be observed or discussed or thought. Gradually our old parental and cultural and familiar (habitual) points of view become a guide to "How to Belong" for them. Gradually, what is "supposed to be" and "supposed to happen" is getting constructed. Who they are and how they fit into this adult world is also getting constructed. Think of what each of the two toddlers in the coffee shop were learning about fitting in.

All these things are but small pieces of what our children begin to discover from the moment of birth onwards. It is learning. It is natural. As they get older, they are also thinking about what they are learning – even philosophical things, as the following true and verbatim story illustrates:

The Meaning of Life – A Pondering

From the back seat of my VW van, on the way back from swimming one summer, I overheard the following exchange between Davy (male) and Alison (female), both about 4½ years old.

Davy (staring out the window): I wonder why there's world.

Alison: Oh, Davy, what are you talking about?

Davy: I wonder why there's a world.

Alison (sighing): So we can play ... so we can have houses.

Davy (slightly exasperated): No, no, I mean I wonder why there's a world.

Alison: So we can have backyards!! Where would we play? Oh David ...

Davy (quiet for a few seconds): ... So we can love each other ...

Alison (deep in thought for a minute or so): ... and have babies!

Learning About Learning

What do our children learn from us about learning itself? What did you learn about learning? Is it hard or easy? Exciting or boring? Useful or a waste of time? Is it something that requires effort, teachers, and schools; or can you learn anything almost anywhere? From our early childhoods and early schooling, we have adopted a lot of myths about learning, reading, talent, hard work, motivation, play, and schooling. Here are some surprising facts to consider:

- We learn more facts about the world from birth to age three than we do from age three until death.
- The older we become, the less conscious we are of what is happening around us (our young children are more aware of the specifics of what is happening at any moment than we parents are).
- It is easier for our brain to learn to read a printed word than learn to identify a color.
- It is just as easy for a young child's brain to learn to read the words "tyrannosaurus rex" as it is for him to learn to read the word "cat."
- If we had learned the concrete language of math, we wouldn't need a $4 calculator (or a paper and pencil) to multiply 239 times 456.
- Most children (with 46 chromosomes) are born with virtually the same cognitive potential.
- Rewards as well as punishment interfere with motivation, learning, and performance.

- A human cortex actually grows (adds neurons) when absorbing lots of new data and new thinking – throughout life.
- Any threat, perceived or real, tends to interfere with cognitive growth, learning, and development.

I didn't make these things up, and believing them isn't required. But you will find that young children's behavior begins to make a lot more sense when we assume these are true. Consider that you have a very able, yet very ignorant (inexperienced), learning machine in your house. And you, in their eyes and in the first couple of years, are the expert – no matter what you think.

III. The Brain, Automaticity, and Behavior

*I*s *it not reasonable that our understanding of the human mind would be greatly aided by knowing the purpose for which it was designed?*

– Willams, George C [16]

If the human brain is so amazing, then why do we keep doing the same things over and over when doing them does not result in what we say we want? If our children are so brilliant, why do they so often seem to thwart our intentions and make day-to-day life so frustrating? To answer these questions, we will examine some of what has been learned about the human brain: what it has been, and continues to be, used for, and why it works the way it does. Our brain, in this part, simply means our "gray matter." Later we will look at a simple breakdown of a many-moduled lump of gray matter as three separate but integrated brains, though more recent research suggests that our brain is more like a system of inter- and intraconnected problem-solving processes, sometimes integrating seamlessly with each other, and sometimes competing with each other.

---

16 William, George C., 1966. Adaptation and Natural Selection. Princeton: Princeton University Press.

Brain Capacity

A young child has roughly 100 billion brain cells (neurons). That would be a computer with 100 GB of RAM if we consider that a neuron is the equivalent of 8 bits. Whether it is or not I have not been able to find out. No matter, though. 100 billion neurons is a lot of neurons. But that is for static, unchanging information. Now let's consider that each one of these neurons can connect with up to 10,000 other ones. What does that mean? From a fact list in the March 2011 issue of the science magazine Discover:

> ***100 trillion*** – *Minimum number of neural connections, or synapses, in the human brain. That is at least 1,000 times the number of stars in our galaxy.*

And from researcher Vilayanur Ramachandran, Director of the Center for Brain and Cognition and a professor in the Neurosciences Graduate Program at UCSD, said during an interview, "When you look at the structure of the brain it us made up of neurons. Of course, everybody knows that these days. There are 100 billion of these nerve cells. Each of these cells makes about 1,000 to 10,000 contacts with other neurons. From this information people have calculated that the number of possible brain states, of permutations and combinations of brain activity, exceeds the number of elementary particles in the universe."[17]

And not only that, it has a characteristic known as neuro-plasticity – it can grow new neurons and change its wiring patterns throughout much of its lifetime. You and I cannot comprehend what this really means about the capability of what lies between our children's ears. I suggest a simple and more useful way to think about this: consider that the capacity of a typical child's brain is unlimited. By considering this to be true, we can be assured that we aren't short-changing

---

17 Ramachandran, V.S., "Mirror neurons and imitation learning...," article on www.edge.org/3rd_culture/

ourselves or our children, and we can focus on what our children are learning instead of wondering whether they are learning.

What is learning, and how does it happen? Our brain is constantly linking (associating) new data (concrete) with old data, determining its usefulness using old and desired future results. It does this automatically, much like and much faster than a computer can create links between subjects, objects, words, etc. We are born doing this, and this is key understanding our children's learning potential as well as what our children have already learned: we do most of it without our conscious awareness. For us parents, with years of experience and associations, we hear the word "apple" and we may visualize an apple (the fruit). We may also visualize our Apple computer, Apple computer logo. We may recollect the tastes and smells of different kinds of apples along with pies, laptops, iPads, our son-in-law who has an iPhone, our daughter baking an apple pie, and on and on. These all involve neuronal links in the brain. You may have heard the axiom, "Neurons that fire together, wire together."[18] This is linking, and linking is a simple process, as we now know from using our internet search engines (finding the specific information we want from a huge database is more complex).

The complexity of what we learn also increases as we build conceptual knowledge, starting with the specific. Though part of our brain sees patterns first, we also see patterns in the patterns, moving from the view of a book, then to it being a collection of pages (sheets of paper with designs), lines of print, then words, each of which has a meaning or function. We are taught to then break words into letters with names and sounds (with lots of exceptions to the rules we were taught in school, remember?).

This is what our children's brains are doing virtually all the time, and mostly behind the scenes. And this is why it doesn't work to grill or

---

18 Wikipedia. Donald O. Hebb.
 http://en.wikipedia.org/wiki/Donald_O._Hebb. Accessed 1/20/11.

test[19] our young children: much if not all of the initial stage of learning happens below their conscious awareness – but they are learning, and at a great rate. The specifics, however, are just not consciously and quickly available. There are also conditions which hinder this constant learning. As parents, this is just as important as seeing how much our children can and do learn very early, and we will consider this later in chapter 5.

Now you may wonder: if the brain's capacity is so large, why may we frequently have difficulty answering a question or coming up with an instant solution to a current problem? One reason why is because we are, as we mentioned earlier with regard to our children, limited in our ability to be consciously aware of large quantities of information and the complexity of the relationships between people, thinking, and concepts. Can you imagine being conscious of every fact, every experience, every concept, you've ever learned? Don't you dislike getting interrupted from something that you are assimilating or when following a complex story or thought process?[20] The idea, that operationally we have a limited "desktop" or "stage" on which the facts, characters, actions, and details of the projects we engage with can be kept in our conscious mind, is dis-cussed by author David Rock in his book, <u>Your Brain at Work</u>.[21] Our limitation of being able to focus on only a relatively small amount operational decision-making data does not mean we don't have the brain capacity to hold far more data than we can imagine. Nor does it mean we must be always be conscious of the all the details involved in the decisions we make. In his fascinating book, <u>Blink</u>, Malcolm Gladwell cites numerous examples of people who made really effective decisions without being consciously aware of the all the data, implications, and possible consequences before they

---

19 That is, ask with some condition or expectation (consequence) attached to giving a right or wrong answer.

20 Do you remember that early on in school, for some, when the bell rang we were disappointed, and later on we couldn't wait for the classroom bell to ring?

21 Rock, David, <u>Your Brain at Work</u>, HarperCollins, 2009.

made them.[22] Less conscious thinking (perhaps that is what we call "intuition") adds to our ability to integrate all the data in our neurological "back rooms," so don't discard quiet time, reflection time, and enjoying art and music. Perhaps that is when most not-conscious, pattern-analysis, and goal-reaching thinking occurs. There are many stories of how significant discoveries happened not in the lab or study group, but in the bathtub, in a dream, or sitting under a tree. Take a moment – how much time like this does your child have during a normal day – especially if she is in school?

Our human brain system is designed to be able to create remarkable relationships. It also must ensure we survive, both as individuals and as a species. And, of course, immediate survival activity trumps conscious, self-directed cognitive learning as well as learning from social activity. Let's begin sorting this out by discussing a few basic facts and functions about the human brain. We will start with this one: our brain is really a system composed of many independent yet integrated "brain modules," not just one. Of the three basic modules we are going to discuss, each one does its own particular kind of "thinking:" it uses data from different sources, has a different agenda, and has its own way of communicating.

For simplicity, I am going to discuss the brain divisions in a somewhat outdated manner, dividing our brain into three distinct parts. Understanding how these three parts operate will begin our exploration of behavior, and how it is related to our feeling and thinking. It explains why we sometimes feel confused or conflicted about what to do or why we (or our spouse, partner, or child) did something and we think, "I thought I (you) knew better!"). It also explains why the behavior of others sometimes makes no sense to us whatsoever, just as our behavior may, at times, make no sense to them. The three parts are the hindbrain, the midbrain, and the cortex. Though each one is composed of several parts, we will look very generally at each one as if it is one unit.

---

22 Gladwell, Malcolm, <u>Blink</u>, Back Bay Books, NY, 2005

Understanding what each of our three brains do can free us from a sense of guilt or a sense that there must be something wrong somewhere, with something we did, or something our child or partner did. To use our driving analogy, if we were driving our car forward by using only the side view mirror, we would experience a kind of frustration much like we experience in our parenting. Why do we keep running into the same barriers? We would think there is something wrong somewhere, wouldn't we? Discovering a front windshield would bring a new view of our situation. And we would make corrections automatically as we drive. Our driving would naturally improve, and we wouldn't settle for or accept our current ability. I am suggesting we shift our intention and attention, as parents, away from what we think we should be doing, feeling, and thinking, and on to what is actually happening in any situation at hand. This, in effect, is turning our head a few degrees and begin using the windshield to see where we are going rather than the side mirror.

Instead of looking at our behavior as if we have one brain and that we should have total control over it, we're going to look at each one of our three brains and focus particularly on two of them, since being unaware of how they work causes most misunderstandings about human behavior. I am not going to go into all the newly discovered fine details of our neurological system (as interesting as it is), but discuss just enough to give us a more practical view of human behavior. This new outlook provides an explanation for our confusion, self-doubt, and successes and failures in dealing effectively with our children's behavior as well as our own.

Our Three "Brains"

The Hindbrain

The first brain we'll examine is our hindbrain (scientific name: rhombencephalon), and though it is composed of three parts: the medulla, pons, and cerebellum, I am going to lump them all together for this section. It is evolutionarily the oldest part of the human brain. It is the only brain that reptiles have and thus is sometimes called our "reptilian brain." Old though it is, it is still fully functional as one of our brains. An example of how it functions is when we perceive we are under attack (for example, being criticized) we act like a snake, and "strike" just as quickly with a look, a biting retort, or even a physical slap or blow. This hindbrain is located behind and under our other two brains. It includes our brain stem, located at the top of our spinal cord. All of our physical sensing neuronal connections feed into our spinal cord, up through our brain stem, and into our hindbrain before going on to much of our higher brain system.

Our hindbrain doesn't need our conscious awareness to decide to act; it just commands us to react. And it basically has two options: fight or flight. It draws from a long history of events and past reactions in order to make instant decisions. How do we know this? The earliest developed manifestations of this function are our reflexes. The "startle" reflex is a good lower brain example: no thinking or conscious awareness is necessary. Our instant reactions to our children's misbehaviors operate just like our reflexes, though many of our parenting behavioral reactions are coming our adopted expectations (List B) rather than deeper threats to physical survival. We immediately react to our children's "bad" behavior (get upset), just like our parents or grandparents reacted to us when we were young – even if we made an earlier decision to not to treat our children the same way. Mostly our reactions don't lead us to anything on our List A (now is a good time to look at your list and verify the last statement from your own experience), but occasionally, and thankfully, our reaction may save our child from severe injury or worse. These reactions come from the past rather than being actions for the future we want. Our hindbrain has no idea of what is on our List A – our future goals. It could care less. It's job is to be sure that we survive threats; that is, stay alive to work toward our List A!

Our hindbrain uses a simple exclusionary 'yes or no,' 'this or that,' or 'you or me,' decision logic when it comes to sensing a "threat" and taking action (fight or flight/hide). We can know we are in this mode of behavior because we will be upset in some way. Being upset is a hindbrain response to something in our environment. And our upsets express themselves over a wide spectrum of behavior, from violent and aggressive behavior to merely an avoidance of a particular person or a rejection of a new idea.

Notice we don't have to be aware of being upset for our hindbrain to influence our thinking and behavior. Whenever we limit our choices to a this-or-that decision it is because of our hindbrain is being efficient for perceived survival purposes, and that may not be helpful in the moment in reaching our parenting goals (again, List A).

Beginning to pay attention to our physical sensations and associated feelings, thoughts, and behaviors at any moment helps us recognize our hindbrain-determined automatic activity, as this brain reacts to our subtle body sensations, familiar thoughts, and recurring feelings associated with our in-the-moment perception of what is happening (changing) in our environment. This is the data that our hindbrain pays attention to, and from which it makes decisions, and not infrequently we go out of control, as the following story illustrates:

"Stop it!!!"

I had a disturbing experience in my second year of working with preschoolers in my late 20's. I was building a garage for a Hot Wheels® car at the Lego® table. Two children were seated at the small round table with me. Alicia was working on a house, and Norman was sitting next to me watching me. After a few minutes, Norman reached over and pulled off a piece of the garage. "Hey!" I said sharply, startling both of us. I paused. Then, relaxing, I asked, "Norman, would you like to help me?"

"No," he replied.

"Will you put back what you took off?"

"No," he said.

"Okay," I said. I went back to work. Before long he reached over and pulled down part of the wall.

"Norman, what's going on?" He just looked at me with a smirk. "Look, you can help me or not, but would you not wreck what I am working on?" I asked. He looked away, and I went back to work on the garage.

A minute later he wrecked another piece of the garage. I grabbed his arm and, in a loud and severe tone, said, "Stop it!!" He was clearly scared. I let go. I froze. Then I looked over at Norman. I said, "Norman, I'm sorry I grabbed you, and yelled at you. Are you okay?" Tears were in his eyes, but he looked at mine and nodded 'yes.' "Did I hurt you?"

He nodded, "yes."

I took a look at his arm. It was red but uninjured. I knew I had grabbed him hard, though, way too hard, and totally unnecessarily. "Norman, I really am sorry." He knew he was okay and was listening. "I got really mad when you were wrecking what was working on. I apologize for yelling and grabbing you. I won't do that ever again. I promise."

He looked in my eyes. His fear appeared gone. I recounted the incident to his mom when she came to pick him up and apologized to her also. Later, I still was a bit shaken. My reaction was clearly not appropriate. Had you asked me beforehand I would have said I clearly understand that is not how to treat a three-year-old, but knowing that made no difference in that moment. The voice that had come out of my mouth, both the words and the tone of it, had shocked me too: it was clearly my father's voice. I had never experienced that before. I began to pay a lot more attention to my emotional state after that, and, while I encountered many other similar situations, I never again unintentionally grabbed or yelled that loudly at any of the children I worked with.

There is one other significant impact on our creative thinking by the hind brain. It limits our options drastically, and being automatic, we don't even notice.

The Law of Opposites

We live in a world defined to a large extent by opposites. Opposites are one of the subjects our children learn early, and opposites are a focus of teaching language in school. An understanding of the Law of Opposites will give us a view of how we tend to have an automatic and limiting way to think about nearly everything in life and how that thinking can have benefits as well as costs. Note that in defining one side of an opposite, the other side is automatically defined. There can be no sense of what "up" means without "down," or "hot" without "cold," "strong" without "weak," etc.

Many of our options with regard to behavior and parenting tend to occur as dichotomies, as opposites, and we look for the 'best' and avoid the 'worst', or search for the 'right' and avoid the 'wrong' choice. This tendency obscures that sometimes one option might work and sometimes another might work. The question itself: "Which is the 'right' choice?" has us focus on something other than our List A desires. Here are some examples of how the Law of Opposites affects our decision-making as well as our assessments (remember List B?) of our children and ourselves; they are hind-brain friendly questions, and the implication is one is right or better than the other.

- Should we be in control of our children, or "let them learn!" (the hard way)?
- Is what they did, or is what I did, good or bad (or right or wrong)?
- Should I be permissive or authoritarian?
- Am I a good parent or a bad parent?
- Should I be a friend to my child, or the enforcer of right behavior?

How useful are these questions? Is there a right answer? Our automatic thinking about each of these, no matter the result, limits our choices and determines our thinking and communication. The Law of Opposites also gets us into debates that distract us. These debates become the drama for talk shows and blogs. For example, with regard to "control," we tend to think, or at least act, as if we should be in control of our children. I recently saw a headlined letter in the newspaper: "Where Are the Parents? Children are out of control …" That debate – to be in control or not – overlooks that sometimes it is necessary to jump in and control our child's behavior, and sometimes it is more valuable to stand back, let them choose, and take the consequences. It always depends on the child, the circumstances, the time constraints, the safety constraints, previous learning, amount of practice, etc. Even our own mood in the moment can make one or even both choices unworkable (more on this in chapter five).

Except in extreme emergencies, we don't have to pick one or the other of these opposites. But thinking that we have to choose one side or the other, or just doing so without thinking, is a prime example of this either/or limitation, determined by that automatic way of thinking we have inherited. We unintentionally limit ourselves to two philosophical options when the solution to our problem is not a philosophical one, it is dependent on time, place, and circumstances. That is, sometimes being in control of our children works, and sometimes letting them make mistakes works – it just depends.

Note, by the way, that although we each have differing specific "triggers" that activate our hindbrain reactions with varying sensitivity and intensity, everyone of us has triggers and thus automatic reactions. It is a part of being human.

The Limbic Brain

Just above our hind brain, in the middle of the neuronal system in our heads, is our limbic brain (including the amygdala). This is also an old brain, developing in the first mammals. It is integrated with the hindbrain and the rest of our body. Its function is to process memory and emotions, and focuses on what physical sensations we are feeling internally. This is key in how we interpret much of our past experience via our hind brain. These interpretations may later be associated in language, becoming the labels we come to know as our "feelings." Thus our limbic brain is considered our "emotional brain." Our pre-verbal interpretations, linked to our past experiences, are one step of complexity above our physical sensations. They are frequently interpreted as threats, prompting automatic or habitual reactions, behaviors, and thoughts (e.g., explanations for behaviors) that are based on or adopted from our past.

The Cortex

Thank goodness we have a third brain – a cortex. Only a cortex can consider the future, and answer the question, "what could I do next?" It can then not only choose an existing option that might work toward something we want (List A), but can actually choose or invent a new option, something that is not one of our strategies (List C). And the only reason it has the time to consider new actions is because its partner, the hind brain, is taking care of all the potentially serious survival threats (our internal "bouncer/body guard"!).

Our cortex is our "creative-thinking" brain. All it needs is a job or goal to accomplish (a future), past and current information, a pause in the action to take in the specifics of a current circumstance and determine whether it is a real threat now or not, and if not, make a choice that matches a goal on List A. The idea of "becoming a child again" may mean re-instituting a process we excelled in when we were young: hypothesize, experiment, fail, re-think, re-hypothesize, experiment again, confirm that it works, and finally use as needed or wanted. That is what your child does so well automatically from birth (as did you and I).

Our goal as parents, then, could be to give our children opportunities to appreciate, exercise, and strengthen the behaviors that we'd like to see emerge. Whether we do this intentionally or not doesn't matter. Whatever behavior best meets the belonging and learning (survival) needs in our child's environment will grow and strengthen, no matter if its origin is genetic or learned. This goes back to your List A. What is important to you? How can you head in the direction of any of your goals while strengthening your child's being loved, supported, and able to contribute? Your cortex will be able to figure this out.

Using Our Brains

We can give instructions to our cortex much like we can give instructions to others, or even to our computer. Recently I asked (searched on Google), "How to Install an Agitator-Dog in a Washing Machine?" and up came a video demonstration. Fortunately, it worked (I did what was shown). I could also say that I first asked my cortex, "Can I do this myself?" And my cortex said, "Maybe ... look online, perhaps YouTube." In life, we say, "I want this – it is important to me," whether it is something we desire in our professional life or whether it is a behavior we want from our child. Our cortex is a problem-solving machine – the "best-ever" when kept clean of garbage (GIGO – garbage in, garbage out). But only when allowed to do its work. It takes into account all kinds of information: what happened in the past, what is desired in the future, what is happening now, what has worked and what hasn't, what hasn't been tried yet, what are the constraints, even what will set off an attack from another person's hindbrain (and this is a useful bit of knowledge to learn to deal with in any relationship!).

Fear keeps us safe without taking up cortex space and time – we don't have to remember what is dangerous every second, and what actions we must take to avoid danger. But using fear as a primary behavioral motivator on our children in general, whether inadvertent or not, limits their learning, growth, and sense of being loved and belonging. They will attempt to get away from the source of fear as soon as they can. Everyone fears punishment (physical harm, pain, and death), and fears being ostracized (exiled, rejected by loved ones, by our family, by our community). Fear also has people do things outside the norm, outside social boundaries, which can be good for society, helping break new ground. Fear triggers the hindbrain to take over, and respond with one of two no-thinking-no-learning-necessary options: fight, or flee (and consider hiding as a fleeing behavior). Fear is the motivator to resort to overt violence and in covert manifestations: hiding (lying, avoiding) and hostility (undermining, sabotaging).

We don't need to use fear as a primary behavioral motivator on our children, and we are used to using it – in very subtle ways. Our children already want the same things we want: to love, belong, learn, and make a difference, to have a job worth doing, and a life worth living. It takes an integrated neural system in a mostly non-threatening environment to accomplish these things.

Fortunately you already have your List A. And if you don't have it, go back to Chapter I – What Do You Really Want, and make your list. You have probably noticed that I keep referring to it, and I will continue to do so. It is worth every bit of your time, and without it, your cortex has no way to know how to use what we are discussing.

You can have conversations in your family about what is important to you. You can invite and encourage others in your family to talk about what is important to them. It just works to do this. At this point, don't worry if they don't like what is on your list, and you don't like anything that is on their list. Just listen. Don't worry about agreeing with or disagreeing with what they want. Just listen and notice everything you want to say about what they say – and don't say anything. And when they are done, just say, "Thank you for letting me know." And smile. It will be okay. We are going to discover a way to talk about what we want and don't want with our children, and how to deal with boundary-crossing behaviors that do not threaten our relationships with them, that do not threaten their own autonomy, and that support intrinsic reasons for cooperation and communication – but we're not there yet.

Our cortex is a problem-solving machine, and it grows and develops through use – that is, by giving it problems to solve instead of trying to avoid them! Note, however: we cannot get our child's cortex make him do what we want or learn what we want him to – only our child can do that. And this, in my view, gets to one of the prob-lems we are not facing in our parent and teacher educational train-ing: when our parental short-term goals take precedence, on a day-to-day basis, over our children's attempts to satisfy their innate drives.

Steven Pinker in his book, The Blank Slate, concludes that:

> *Behavior is not just emitted or elicited, nor does it come dir-ectly out of culture or society. It comes from an internal struggle among mental modules with differing agendas and goals.*[23]

Now do we see why we may frequently feel confused, shameful, second guess ourselves, and desperately want to find "the right" answer? We are attempting to balance our needs and desires with our children's drives and desires. They will never be in balance, except by chance. We address each one as it comes up, and our needs, in many ways, take priority, just like the airlines advise us to put on our own oxygen masks before we put on our children's. We do one thing at a time; multi-tasking – consciously – is a myth. Yet, when we take good care of ourselves, we are also making ourselves more able to take good of our children. And our children learn that taking good care of themselves is what it means to be an adult (or, if your child is young, to be a Big People).

Noticing our own behavior and reactions reveals our conflicting agendas and engages our cortex. When we then face a decision about what to do next, we can think about what we have done in the past, we choose based on several agendas: Is this the time? Is this the right (or wrong) choice? Am I undermining my child's trust? Am I being a pushover? And, by the way, this is important:

---

23 Pinker, Steven, The Blank Slate: The Modern Denial of Human Nature, Vik-ing, 2002, p 40.

Whether you take time for reflective assessment just before an emotional outburst (hindbrain reaction), sometime during one, or sometime after one, your cortex still gets exercised. Virtually all of us feel guilty or bad after we have done something we think we "shouldn't" have, such as yelling at our two-year-old, or even our teen. I am saying: notice that feeling, and then, replace the thought with, "Oops ... there goes (or there went) my hindbrain ... thank goodness I have one!"

A summary of the purposes and functions of the three brains is available in Appendix II, page 203.

IV. Memory, Emotions, and Meaning

*I*t's *no wonder that truth is stranger than fiction. Fiction has to make sense.*

— *Mark Twain*

Memory

My eldest daughter, Brynn, and I were talking about Halloween costumes from our past – I think she was in high school at the time, and at that time we were talking about our memories of them. She said she remembered being dressed up as a raccoon and carrying a green plastic bag. But in a more recent conversation, she said she noticed that her last memory of that particular event, the costume and setting, matched exactly a picture in one of our scrapbooks, and that she didn't recall any other memories of that event. She said, "Maybe I wasn't remembering the event but was instead remembering the picture in the scrapbook that I looked at later." That is very possible, even likely, and the following explains why.

Research suggests that the first time we recall an event, we are rerunning a neural program circuit of past associations. Brynn, in the following example, was recalling Halloween, raccoon, green bag of candy, and trick or treating. This was the circuit Brynn ran on her very first recollection of the event. Later, another association (link) occurred: a photograph in a scrapbook seen several times and several years after the event. The photograph seemed exactly the same as the visual memory in her head. She noticed that, and questioned her own memory. Was it a memory of the actual event, or was the memory from looking at the photograph?

When we recall a past event, we assume that the details of it are pretty accurate. But over time we may well have added some new data from later that has also become linked to the event. Each time the experience is recalled and before we move on, it is "saved" much like saving a file on our computer. The first time we save the file, it just saves it under a name – let's say <Brynns Raccoon Halloween>. But after the second recollection, when we see the message, "<Brynns Raccoon Halloween> already exists. Replace it?", and on our computer, we get to choose. Not so with our memory, says Dr. Kareem Nader, a neuroscientist at McGill University. Our brain appears to save the latest recollection of a memory, after incorporating and modifying the information with new images, conversations, and others' recounted recollections of the event, writing over the earlier file named <Brynns Raccoon Halloween>.[24] There is no longer an original <Brynns Raccoon Halloween>. Daniel J Siegel describes the process of remembering as "the construction of a new neural net profile with features of the old engram [original incident] and elements of memory from other experiences, as well as influences from the present state of mind."[25] In either view of the slightly differing descriptions of the process, our memories are not what we think. They are not totally accurate and unbiased "original recordings" of past events. They are modified to fit our "life stories" – they are very related to our view of ourselves, our circumstances, and existing beliefs – and all these are related to the survival of who we think we are.

---

24 WNYC's RadioLab, "Memory and Forgetting," June 8, 2007.
25 Siegel, Daniel J, The Developing Mind, Guildford Press, 1999, p28.

Right now I'm having amnesia and déjà vu at the same time. I think I've forgotten this before.

— Steven Wright, comedian

Stephen Wright's humorous comment has a lot of validity. Our new view of how memory works has huge yet subtle ramifications, yes? Think of the arguments and upsets we have experienced with each other over differing memories of the same event! Perhaps we should be suspicious when we agree with our child or spouse about the details of, or someones intentions during, a past event!

Have you ever wondered why young children seem very confident and accurate about past events, a least when very young? Being young, with "fresh" neurons and fewer overwrites, makes this is a plausible explanation.

Those of us who understand verbal language have two kinds of memory, and there is a significant difference between the two. Being aware of this difference also can help us make sense of a lot of behavior that seems to make no sense to us.

Implicit Memory

We now know, through research and, perhaps from our own experience, that young children, even babies, are able to "recall" past experiences. In babies, these recollections take the form of emotional reactions and behaviors. If our baby has been scared by a loud and sudden noise made by a truck going by and saw the truck, she may get upset whenever a truck approaches. When I made the sound of an elephant trumpeting, my older daughter thought it was funny when she was a baby, but her younger sister acted terrified of it, perhaps because I startled her when I first did it. I found out later that even when I told her I was going to do it, and then did it, she would still get upset. While she is no longer terrified of it (she was twenty-three at the time of my writing this), she still doesn't like recalling her memory of my doing it. Furthermore, she has never had any explanation for why she doesn't like it. This is the nature of a memory linked to something that occurs or is absorbed before we acquire language. As Daniel Siegel writes, "(We) act, feel, and imagine without any recognition of the influence of past experience on our present reality."[26] That is, we don't remember learning or experiencing these memories. They reside in our "perceptual memory," but not in our "thought memory." This kind of memory is called "implicit memory." What makes this extremely significant in human behavior is that, without any memory of having learned something, we then automatically act as if that that memory, be it visual, auditory, sensory, or attitudinal, is "the truth," no matter that we may encounter evidence to the contrary. These implicit memories can determine our current feelings, attitudes, and behaviors in general as well as under certain circumstances which are similar to the circumstances when we created them. Whether we think a memory is the truth or not can lead to family arguments and even relational breaks, as our hindbrain is determining that there is a threat to us. Mostly, we can avoid this by saying, "That is what I remember – what do you remember?" and listen. Our allowing differing memories to co-exist as valid memories is not threatening – unless there are significant elements that must be dealt with for health, safety, and/or legal reasons.

One way to recognize that our behavior as a parent is originating from these early memories, without having to figure out what the original learning incident was, is to notice when our current behavior is antithetical to what we know to do, or is inconsistent with our beliefs, or persists when we don't want it to. When we cannot determine why we acted as we did – that is, we cannot recall learn-

---

26 Siegel, Daniel J., <u>The Developing Mind</u>, The Guilford Press (1999), p.29

ing to behave that particular way and a result of what we did was unintentional – we could assume that it came from our implicit memory. We can infer that we learned it because we do it without deciding ahead of time. My story "Stop It!" (page 51) is a good example of the relationship between our automaticity and our implicit memory. Are we bad parents or teachers when we react with anger, force, or disappointment? Don't we "know better"? Sure – when we take time to think. Telling ourselves that we "know better" doesn't help us any more than it helps saying that to our children. And no, we are not bad parents when we react with anger or disappointment. The science says (and likely your intuition too) that our reactions are not due a lack of our commitment to, or a lack of love for, our children.

Attempting to follow the common parenting advice, "control your emotions," is not practical even if eventually possible. Our emotional outbursts are not a personal flaw, but a natural hindbrain function, a result of being "triggered." It is not that we are being bad parents when we react. We react because we are human, and all humans have hindbrain triggers. The view that something, or someone, is wrong when people get angry is likely learned before we are three. It is in our implicit memory. We can feel bad or insufficient or powerless and we don't really know why, and that causes additional stress.

What is most important to our children ("under the radar") is that which makes them feel safe, loved, and secure in belonging with us. That is, that they are confident that we will never reject or leave them, satisfying their innate drive to belong. And, as we have discussed, when we get upset, our message to them is threatening. From a very youngest child's view, whenever we, the parents, are upset, it has something to do with them. It has to. It happens in their world, and they haven't yet learned that who they are is just a tiny, imperfect, and insignificant piece in a huge world, and that human beings, by physical appearance and cultural definition, are separate from each other. But in a year or so, they will be living by those newly learned rules, and some years after that, those rules too become automatic. Little or no thinking (by the higher level cortex) is required to live by them.

Explicit Memory

Now for the second kind of memory: explicit memory. Compared to implicit memory, this is easy: any behavior, feeling, or thought that you recall that you learned is from explicit memory. When you use the new information you learn in this book, or remind yourself of the items on your Lists A, B, or C, or consciously choose some old or new strategy on your List C, you are using data from explicit memory.

Emotions

Every healthy human being experiences a wide range of emotions, each of which are part of the experience of being human. The idea that specific ones are "good" feelings and some are "bad" feelings was, and may still be, taught to us by our parents and/or in school – either directly or by implication (especially via facial expression). Also, whether because of genetics or early experiences or some combination, some feelings are desirable – they feel good. We want them. Some make us uncomfortable and uncertain. We don't want those to persist. And some we do not like or want to feel at all – they "make" us feel strongly that we are not in control, or are bad or wrong. Given what we have discussed so far, these threatening "negative" feelings could easily have been learned in our very early years and reside in implicit memory: the feeling itself is perceived as bad or wrong, rather than the likelihood that the current circumstance has triggered a past association of threat of loss of love and belonging. No matter the source, however, our wide range of emotional experience is what makes us human, normal, and adds diversity (novelty). Telling or acting, as parents or teachers, as if some feelings themselves are good and some are bad, is like teaching our children that some of their bones are good and some are bad, and they should only have the good ones!

Typically our children learn, both implicitly and explicitly, how one should feel when certain circumstances happen: you are sad when you move away from friends or when your pet rabbit dies, for example. Of course we are, and we don't really need to "teach" this. But many times there are pre-existing emotional conditions that can make simple dictums very confusing for children and that confusion can last well into adulthood.

Stuffed Emotions

A very dear friend and close relative of mine came to me several years after her husband of over 35 years had died of cancer. She said that she wanted to tell me about something, and that she hadn't yet shared it with anyone else because she felt very guilty about it. She added that she hadn't felt that she had grieved the way she should have or wanted to. What she said was that she felt a tremendous sense of relief when her husband died, and not because she didn't love him. He had been very controlling and had frequently refused to talk about what she wanted or suggested. "Count your lucky stars," he'd reply when she complained. She had been very unhappily married for many years and his death brought her a sense of freedom.

Why did she feel guilty about this? She had come to believe (learned), likely starting from her parents, that people should feel loss and sadness at the death of someone whom they have loved and with whom they have lived for many years, and if they didn't, there must be something wrong. After she had told me about her guilt and some details of her marriage, she then considered that, given her circumstances, of course she would feel a sense of relief. It didn't mean she didn't love him. And she could finally grieve.

How do our children learn about emotions from us? As with virtually all early learning, they learn from our emotional self-expression and what we then say or don't say about it – how we explain our emotional expression, but only if we do that – as they are learning language.

How do we avoid passing on our early-learned negative judgments of certain emotions? We can't and won't avoid it much of the time. But we can pay attention to and talk about our emotions and judgments as we encounter them – we can talk about how we feel about our feelings. It is normal to feel bad when we have emotions that we think we shouldn't have. This is an internal emotional entanglement, a double-whammy. We can, however, after noticing our own feelings about our feelings, talk about them in a way that helps our children to view emotions as part of being human. We are "talking-for-learning" when we share our own realizations and feelings, letting our children know it is common to feel sad and even angry over a significant loss, or for us to feel angry when things don't go the way we want or expect. We can, in our telling our stories, have our children feel okay when they feel different than others think they should feel under any circumstance. We can never feel different than the way we feel at any moment. This is different than "teaching" our children "about" emotions, like painting a picture in front of a child and talking about the experience and unfolding of it is very different than being "taught how to paint." Everyone feels and every feeling is valid. But communicating feelings through words is another thing.

Is it really possible to tell someone else what one feels?

— Anna Karenina, by Leo Tolstoy

Over-emphasizing that our children verbalize their feelings "accurately" can lead to frustration and our child not feeling "heard." Listening to verbal emotional expressions with all of our senses, and not trying to teach a right way to verbalize allows our children more freedom to be themselves. Letting our children experiment with the verbal descriptions, which, as Tolstoy's character questions, leads to being both heard and may encourage a more poetic expression.

In our parenting, I am suggesting that we first consider our emotional reactions as evidence that we are healthy functioning human beings rather than evidence that there is something wrong with us. Wouldn't we be more likely to then consider how to show our feelings without threatening anyone, especially our children?

Now let's consider that it is what we think those reactions mean that determines our resulting behavior.

Meaning

The making of meaning is another significant function of our cortex that plays into our role both as a Big People in our young children's lives. This automatic activity of the brain is also about quick survival behavior. Instantly "knowing" what someone's behavior means – that is, what their intention is – gives us a heads-up on a defensive or offensive protective strategy. Some meanings of things seem innate, and others are learned early. What is key here is to notice we, if asked, automatically usually have a reasonable explanation for (or meaning of) every behavioral event in our lives. We don't typically explore the source for these explanations, we just "jump" to our conclusions. Frequently they tend to be the old familiar ones, the ones we've heard and used over and over. This is yet another example of the influence of the past on our thinking and behavior. But so much is new in our culture, in our knowledge, and thus our thinking and communication. All is changing so fast now that our first explanation, based on the past, always bears questioning. And the first (reactive) explanation is especially problematic when we assume we know another person's intention behind their behavior.

We might think that knowing the meaning of (or motivation for) a specific action on the part of another person comes from our experience in living life with other people. This makes good sense, but there is a common underlying assumption we make, and it is that "we can tell" what some action or response means. We aren't aware that: 1) due to the nature of implicit memory, 2) our hind brain's this-or-that immediate response, and 3) the past-based, automatic meaning-making function of our cortex, our perfectly reasonable explanations may be totally erroneous. And then we, as Big People, pass these "reasons" on to our young children. Since they don't know yet what it means when daddy yells at mommy, they watch us and listen to us. They watch our faces, tones of voice, and gestures, and hear our verbal language, linking all these together with the emotional patterns of the circumstances under which our anger occurred. This plays out throughout our lives. Here is how this played out for me one afternoon:

The Staff Meeting

I was directing a small center of three classrooms in Arlington, Virginia, for a year or so as we trained a new director for it. I had a good relationship with the staff at the center — they were so open to learning and making a difference in the children's lives that I was inspired. But one Monday morning I came in and said good morning and something didn't feel right. I didn't get much eye contact and didn't feel welcomed at all. What did that mean? My first thought was I had hired the wrong staff. My second thought, which I thought was more likely, was that I must have forgotten to do or acknowledge something important. Then I had the feeling that I was failing as a director. I wanted to go home!

Fortunately, I had good training, and I knew it would work to get to the bottom of this as fast as possible no matter how badly I might have screwed up. So I called a meeting with the senior staff at nap time.

After the children were quiet we got together. I started by saying I had noticed when I came in that it didn't feel very open and that no one had greeted me or even made eye contact. They were quiet. So I asked, "Did I forget something? Did I do something or not do something that I had said I would or that you were expecting?" They remained silent. "Uh oh," I thought. "It must have been pretty bad."

Then I said, "I know when I'm upset with someone, I don't want to talk about it. But talking about it and clearing it up is what makes this the best environment for these children ... we are all learning, myself included. So what's up?"

Finally one of them said, "Mr. Marty, on Friday, when you left, you didn't say goodbye to any of us, and you looked upset ... I even saw you roll your eyes." I tried to remember leaving on Friday afternoon. I did leave earlier than usual. Oh, yes ...

I said, "Ms. Betsy, thank you for saying that. I had gotten a call from the central office and they told me I was needed to close the Reston Center because the director was ill. I really didn't want to drive out to Reston and be there until 7 PM last Friday, and I was upset and did leave quickly and hoped nobody would notice." I paused. "I'm sorry I didn't explain that to anyone ... I just wanted to leave and not talk to anyone. I'm sorry that I left you with no explanation."

"Oh," another one of my senior teachers began, "we thought you were upset with us because we brought the children in from the playground a little late and a parent was really mad. But there was a good reason ..."

As she spoke, I could immediately feel myself relax and lighten up, even though I hadn't heard about the upset parent, and I smiled.

"Wow. I thought you were upset because I had done something wrong and you thought I was upset because I thought you had done something wrong. Thank you for being willing to say what was going on ... that always makes a difference."

Note how we all jumped to a conclusion that we had done something "wrong." Why don't we all assume we did something really well when we don't know? Aren't we frequently just waiting for something to go "wrong"? And how long might this misunderstanding have continued had I not called everyone together to find out? Can you recall a problem between family members or friends that has persisted for years, and to you it seems really silly? Isn't the problem really that the two people refuse to talk to each other? Why is that? Don't they have a really good reason for not being willing to talk to the other one? Have you noticed that these misinterpretations can last for days, weeks, and even years?

Let's now look a little deeper. We usually don't deliberately choose to make up meanings. We may ask ourselves, "What does this mean?" to raise our awareness or to deal with a threatening action, and the answer, especially the first answer, is likely to be there already. That is because there is a specific area of the cortex whose job it is to make up meanings for everything that happens. "Making meaning" out of events is like breathing, and these meanings include explanations and justifications. Gossip is typically a sharing of assumed meanings for the behaviors of others, and is rarely, if ever, positive. This meaning-making part of our cortex, in the prefrontal cortex, does not (and cannot) say what the "true" meaning is – it first just makes up what is most reasonable based on what it has absorbed and/or adopted to date. Doesn't the word "reasonable," to you, really mean "within your reason"? If so, doesn't that mean that, at least initially, our reasoning is based on our past experience and learning, on what we have already learned and adopted? Our initial reasons and explanations, at times of surprise, upset, or threat, are just another protective aspect of our reactive hindbrain.

Thus, after being upset and making decisions, it might be more useful to take a moment and just notice what meaning we have attributed to what just happened, and that it is not necessarily the truth. That pause and that consideration, can give our cortex a chance to override a disempowering automatic meaning and make up something that will lead us to our A List, one that not only takes the past into account, but also allows for a new future. When behaviors persist, this is where to look. In doing so, you will begin to see new possibilities and opportunities.

Meanings (aka interpretations) matter to our children's sense of security, sense of belonging, and sense of ability. When a parent says, "I can't play with you now," it can be interpreted many ways by our young and inexperienced children. That statement could mean, "Daddy doesn't want to play with me", or, "playing is not important." It could also mean, "Daddy doesn't love me", and therefore "I am not worthy of love (or even attention)." These are only a few possible internal interpretations on a spectrum of a child's sense of security in belonging. Hopefully, what we usually mean is, "I'd love to play with you, but I have a promise to do something else right now, and someone is depending on me to get that done. I will find a time to play with you as soon as I am finished. I love you!" Having written that possible meaning, it's not just about the words but also about the way it is said. You may not need to add "I love you," for example, but if you can see that your child is feeling rejected or unimportant, adding that as a heart-felt declaration puts your child's sense of belonging back in place. When you mention your other commitment(s), your child begins to see that other people are important, and life is not merely about them. Do you see how valuable your role is in helping your child understand the meaning(s) of what we say and do? Telling our child the whole story, though taking a few seconds longer, could make a huge difference in our child's sense of worthiness and belonging, not to mention that it demonstrates a high level of open communication, trust, and responsibility. Your child will gain confidence in and respect for you.

Interpretations we make about our own behavior as well as our child's behavior have a huge influence on our satisfaction and self-worth as parents. Take a minute and read through your List B again. What has this list meant to you about your parenting? Is it evidence of how able or unable, sufficient or insufficient, or good or bad, you have been as a parent? How do you feel about yourself with regard to your parenting when one of these things is or isn't going the way you want or the way you think it should? How have your feelings been determined by the meanings you have had about certain actions, responses, and behaviors? "I must be lazy," "He was trying to get even," or "I forgot again ... I guess I'm not (good enough, committed, etc.)." Rather than attempt to change your feelings, try re-thinking what those behaviors might have meant: "Something else distracted me...," or "I might have felt some fear..." combined with "I'm a normal human being with normal considerations and distractions. I see... I just keep going and (do my best, get support, take a course, etc.)." Consider that it is possible that none of the meanings (reasons) you have used to explain your parenting "mistakes" are true. Even whether something was a mistake is a meaning that may not be useful as "that was a step that didn't work – I learned something," or, "I keep trying to do this on my own... I will talk about it with Joe and get some feedback."

The meanings we automatically attach to misbehavior[27], when acted upon as true, usually reinforce our current reality: our opinions about our children, about parenting, about our parenting, and about ourselves. Common reasons for "mis"-behaviors that we parents have adopted include "she's tired" and "he's hungry." These are so common that for some, they are unquestionable. My wife, Carolyn, and I tried not to use these reasons with our children when they

---

27 Notice that the word "misbehavior" has a judgmental meaning already embedded within it, as do other words in our language.

were whiny or having a meltdown. Many parents automatically say and accept that being "cranky" means a child is hungry or tired, no matter if they know the child, recent circumstances, or existing behavioral patterns. Certainly a child might be hungry, or might be tired. It might also mean that he is bored with the current options he has, or wants a moment to reconnect with us and we are ignoring him. It might mean that he has not learned to tell us in gestures or words what he wants. What happens to us, adults, when we cannot find the words to say something we want to say? Do we glower or complain, or make a gesture of frustration? When our child continues whining or crying or constantly interrupting us, after we have demonstrated an alternative, that behavior might have become a habitual and legitimate (i.e., learned) way for our child to try to get what he wants.

Children learn to do whatever works from their their two- or three- or four-year-old point of view. But don't we, as adults, also do (or attempt to do) what works from our adult point of view? And isn't what works for us and our children largely dependent on the meanings we each associate with the actions we are encountering, both our own actions and those of others?

Consider this: We assume that certain events that happened in the past determine our behavior ("made me do" or "made me feel") now. But we are discovering that what those events have meant to us – the meaning of them – has a stronger impact on our relational and social behavior today than the events themselves. But if we can come to understand those certain events differently, if we can change what those events have meant to us (since we cannot change what happened), then we have a powerful tool for changing today's behavior. We can say that the meaning we adopt as the reasons for past behaviors, both our own and others', is what determines the quality of behavior around us in the present.

Here is an example: Have you ever noticed that you and a classmate had very different experience of a certain teacher's way of teaching when you were in school? Your friend might have said, "Miss Jones is really mean... she never gives me a break." And you are thinking, "Actually, she is very fair and seems to always being willing to help someone when they ask." Or, have you ever had a parent or grandparent tell you about what one of your parent's life was like when they were a child, and you came to a new understanding of the way that parent treated you, maybe even shifted it from a complaint to a new appreciation? That is the power we have, thanks to the way our cortex functions: using language, communicating with others, rethinking our old thoughts (called metacognition), and gaining a new insight or appreciation for something or someone. You give this power to your child when you share how you learned to do what you do, and the way your mother or father parented you, and when you ask, "What do you think Aunt Joannie might have meant by that comment? What else might she have meant?"

Don't you often wonder why your child misbehaves? That is, what does your child's behavior mean, anyway? If you cannot come up with a meaning that helps, then ask. Or ask regardless. Asking someone what they mean when you aren't sure shows a great deal of respect for who they are.

V. Upsets and Learning

We cannot solve our problems using the same thinking we used when we created them.

— Albert Einstein

Why aren't all children excelling in reading, writing, and mathematics? And why is managing our children's behavior such a daunting challenge, one in which we frequently encounter failure — at least in the goal of getting cooperation without punishment or threat of punishment? It is certainly not because children are not intelligent enough, or are evil, or that teachers are not committed enough. There are other more parent-user-friendly reasons.

Let's start with being upset. Note: I didn't mean for you to get upset right now, but I do want you to begin to notice what happens just before you get upset over something. And consider, given how our hindbrain functions, that whenever we encounter anything new or different, there is a high potential for having an upset occur at any moment, at some level.

The Nature of Upset

Upset *n. An internal emotional disturbance, disorder, or state of agitation frequently resulting in an expressive outburst or an attempt to withhold communication.*

From a scientific point of view, an upset is experienced because of a release of certain chemicals in our hind brain. The effect of these chemicals, according to neuroscientist Jill Bolte, lasts about 90 seconds. Our upsets frequently last longer, and can even last for years. Why is this? It is because the upset trigger keeps being pulled: we may continue an emotional argument or conversation, regardless of whether it is with the same person, another person, or just in our own head. When a person is upset, her hindbrain is running the show. There is no thinking going on, no considering a future outcome. There is only a fight-or-flight reaction. This is why trying to deal with the reasons for our child's or partner's upset when either we or they are still upset rarely, if ever, works.

To relate to someone who is upset, we must find a way to let the chemicals dissipate. We must either walk away (if neither calms down) or, if we calm down first, begin listening to the still-upset person with compassion, allowing them a safe-haven for the expression of the emotions triggered with the upset. This listening "action" can stop the re-triggering event and allow a reflective moment. Then both partners can begin recognizing the past memories, comments, or actions that served to trigger the upset. That points to an important role we can play as parent.

When a parent gets upset around her own child, her young child's hindbrain goes on red alert. For a young child, a parental upset is not merely a loss of love in the moment, but also because a young child considers himself the cause of the parental upset, a potential loss of ongoing support. But what triggers an upset to begin with? See if the following is true in your experience.

I get upset when:

1. I don't get what I want when I expect it, or
2. when what I don't expect and don't want does happen, or
3. when I am misunderstood. (I don't get the understanding that
   I expect, a version of number 1.)

The short version for us is this: We get upset whenever an expectation, conscious or not, is either not met or something appears to
thwart its being met.

> **Expectation** *n. A strong desire for or belief that some
> specific event will occur or goal will be achieved at or by a
> specific time.*

We have tended to think that our upsets are caused by our children's
behaviors. But now consider that it is our *expectations* that have a
more direct influence on our getting upset than our child's behavior.
If you and I can modify our expectations (a big if, I admit, at the
moment), then we can eliminate, or at least decrease, our upsets
without having to change our children's behavior. New relevant
information, one goal of this chapter, can change our view of what
the causes of behaviors are, and thus change our expectations, and
that is a part of a solution for lessening upsets and thus conflict
within our families. While that is definitely valuable, I assert that it is
not necessary to stop getting upset to gain cooperation from your
child without force and be in charge of what happens in your family
– all at the same time. That is our goal.

Now let's attempt to look at upsets from our child's point of view.
Our initial parental upsets are frequently total surprises to our
young child – there is no way our very young children can know all
of our expectations. But they will and do learn them quickly. And,
rightly so, they do not consider it their job to keep us from getting
upset (they would need to meet all of our expectations), but neither

do they think it is their job to make us upset (though we may act as if both are true, at least in their view). In the early years, they are just doing exactly what they should be doing – learning – while also attempting to secure their belonging and support from us. It is when they cannot figure out how to avoid our criticism, disappointment, anger, disapproval, and hypocrisy (do as I say, not as I do) – followed by resentment and sense of powerlessness – that seemingly intentional upset-causing behavior occurs and recurs. Our view that their behavior is often intentional (consciously chosen) leads us to direct our upsets at them, when in fact it is their innate drive for and focus on experimenting and exploring (their "work") that thwarts our expectations at those times. Persisting unsatisfied innate drives cause disruption. You know this: what happens to behavior when desires for hunger or thirst are not met? When socially acceptable ways of satisfying a drive do not work, non-acceptable ways will be attempted, and attempted again and again.

Many if not most of our recurring upsets occur in our closest relationships. And, of course, these are the people we know well. We have strong expectations of them to relate to us in certain ways, and behave in certain ways. And likewise, they of us. That is, both sets of hindbrains are familiar with the patterns of responses within the family. When one behaves in an unexpected way, however, the other hindbrain reacts with a subtle fight-or-flight related response, somewhere on a spectrum from withdrawal (including getting quiet), to an accusation of inconsistency, or to having an emotional outburst (attack). Whether or not we want this kind of response, this is a normal and healthy human behavioral response to unexpected change. You can count on it. Now, begin to notice it when it happens. There is nothing wrong with hindbrain reactions – it is how we all work.

While our own and our children's expectations and upsets play a large role in our behavior, so do our innate drives, as mentioned earlier. This is not new information in the field of human behavior.

Temple Grandin, in her fascinating book, <u>Animals Make Us Human</u>[28], draws upon her own experience and upon the work of Dr. Jaak Panksepp at Washington State University, regarding other causes of behavioral disruption. Panksepp distinguishes what he calls the core emotions – the "Blue Ribbon Emotions." Four of these are key in our discussion now, as they also trigger the hindbrain.

The first one is called "Seeking." It is the impulse to find, investigate, experiment with, and make sense of the world around us. It seems to be a combination of curiosity, desire, and gathering information about anything we don't already know. It is satisfying, and usually pleasurable. This one I have referred to as "the drive to learn, to explore, to grow up as fast as possible," or, as Joseph Chilton Pearce, author of <u>Magical Child</u>, calls it, "the model imperative."[29]

The second is called "Rage." Its evolutionary origin is a survival response to being captured, restrained, or held by a predator, and it gives rise to a huge burst of energy and strength in order to escape. We, in our culture today, are rarely captured by predators to be eaten, but this emotion is nonetheless stimulated when we are restrained or threatened with restraint by a parent or other physically more powerful person of authority. Panksepp says this response is evident at birth: "When you hold a human baby's arms to his sides, he will become furiously angry."[30] I think we may be seeing this more frequently than we think. If this is indeed an innate impulse, consider that when you have to restrain your child and she struggles furiously, it is not her conscious personal "will" that you are experiencing but an automatic and natural human response. Perhaps even the resentment, frustration, and disruptive behavior many children display in school can be explained by the natural

---

28 Grandin, Temple, *Animals Make Us Human*, Mariner Books, 2009, pp 5-9.
29 Pearce, Joseph C, <u>Magical Child</u>, pp (fr Parent workshop on CD).
30 Grandin, Temple, *Animals Make Us Human*, Mariner Books, 2009, pp 5-9.

response to a restrictive and limiting environment, with further stress caused by our parental implicit acceptance of it.[31]

"Fear," the third emotion, we have already discussed. It is clearly an automatic survival-oriented feeling – thus also natural and expected under perceived threatening conditions, "from the physical to the mental and social."[32]

The fourth, "Panic," is what Dr. Panksepp applies to our social attachment system. "All baby animals and humans cry when their mothers leave, and an isolated baby whose mother does not come back is likely to become depressed and die."[33] This is consistent with the latest research on attachment theory and our children's need to belong and be loved unconditionally.

These four emotions arise in the hindbrain and amygdala (part of the limbic brain), are underlying all of our other systems, including our other emotions, our thoughts, and our behaviors.

Upsets cause problematic behaviors, and as we have seen, we seem to have little control over some of the circumstances that cause us to get upset. Now we turn to a conundrum in our relationship with our children, and our children's relationship with us. It is a dilemma that has been explained away rather than dealt with.

---

31 That is, acceptance without a meaningful explanation.
32 Grandin, Temple, Ibid
33   Ibid

The Children's Dilemma

This dilemma occurs as a conflict between the two innate drives:

1. The drive to belong (be loved unconditionally).
2. The drive to explore, experiment, predict, and test (i.e., learn and master life skills).

We have examined how the drive to belong is always operating, whether consciously or not, and that an extraordinary amount of learning can occur in a short time given the capacity and the efficient way in which humans learn. (Our view of this has become clouded by how slowly the content in school is covered). Now let's look at how we, usually unintentionally, distract a child's focus, and inadvertently interrupt one or both of the two innate and essential human drives. The key to this is noticing both how we relate to our children in general and specifically: how we deal with them when they cross boundaries or break our rules. That is, when we are upset.

Think about this: when we get upset, what does our child see and hear? Our face changes, our tone changes, our posture changes, and words of admonition, blame, and threat fly out of our mouths. In these moments, what messages are we giving our child with regard to love and belonging? Do we see, in those moments, our child's sense of being loved and continuing to belong (be wanted) is not being communicated, that something is in the way of our love being perceived? What our child may sense is that we are, in the moment, *unhappy and unsatisfied, perhaps angry, and all that is her fault.* Until our child learns otherwise, in word and deed (that is, through all our languages), the meaning of our getting upset is that she is loved conditionally, and may not continue to be wanted by us.

Given this, your child is left with three options:

1. Continue to experiment and make you upset (withhold your love and caring).
2. Stop experimenting, exploring, and testing (i.e., stop learning).
3. Hide. Hide her thinking, feelings, questions, and concerns, and anything she is considering doing.

Option number one is not possible because of the magnitude of the *survival threat to a young child of the loss of a parent's love and support*. Option number one may appear to be modifiable; that is, our child could reduce the amount of experimenting, but for young children especially, experimenting and exploring is their natural and predominant activity. Any reduction could have a huge negative impact on current as well as future cognitive development, as that development is cumulative. Option number two is not possible – it is the primary activity of a human brain – automatically. The degree to which can a child can tolerate parental upset varies, but in any case there is a huge impact, over time, with any slowing or loss of the development of language, thinking, and motor skills. Option number three, hiding (being secretive, sneaky), is the only strategy that can currently ameliorate the impacts of options one and two. We all adopted that strategy very early, and withdrawal from communication is a big part of what makes hiding easier.

There is a huge cost in relationship with the strategy of hiding. Every time it is used, there is a further reduction in communication, a further reduction in a sense of trust and intimacy. In addition, the more the strategy is used, the more automatic and unnoticed it becomes. It is no wonder that it seems so many parents don't really know about certain aspects of their children's interests and activities, and may be shocked or in disbelief to hear about something their child has done.

When a child cannot figure out how to hide her behavior, (perhaps hiding is not possible with one hovering parent at home, or in a group home situation), she may just decide (a subtle hindbrain decision) to constantly upset her parent, or totally withdraw. Some call the former a "conflict disorder" or a "high conflict personality," and this behavior will keep her parent engaged. The latter, total withdrawal, also results in a great deal of parental concern attention. Some alternating combination of upsetting a parent and hiding may also occur.

Please be clear that I am not saying that parents are to blame for their children's behavior. This will become apparent as we progress.

All of us have encountered The Children's Dilemma, and we have mastered the strategies we found that worked best for us, in our view, at the time. Now our children, depending on their age, are at various stages in developing sophisticated strategies to hide their possibly-upset-causing explorations and experiments from us. We don't realize how much our children's hiding strategy costs us, nor how much they miss out on because of our strategies ("I can't tell my kids about that!").

Think about this: Do you see how, and how much, you hid from your parents as you grew up? Do you remember the first time you told your mom or dad about something you did, and the #*&@% hit the fan? Did you tell them the next time? After telling them about something else later and getting the same result, didn't you stop telling them about a lot things you were thinking and doing? And by high school you were quite good at it, weren't you? What is it like for those of us who have older children, and they have secrets or secret parts of their lives that are hidden from us? Some parents may say, "I'm glad I don't know!" Yes, we don't want to worry. We do love our children. But we also, to some degree, begin to feel distant, irrelevant, powerless, or unfulfilled as a parent. And we'll justify those feelings, saying "it is normal", "it is to be expected", "it is good for our children to become distant – otherwise they'd never go out on their own." I have heard many parents and a few parent educators say this, and nothing could be farther from the truth. (If you think relational distance between a parent and child is natural and good, re-read "In the Coffee Shop," page 36).

How can we break up this cycle? Do we have to rewire our whole system? Fortunately, no. Fortunately, we can use how our brains work, along with a bit of new information: the plasticity of the brain throughout life. It is never too late to grow new or reuse neural pathways. For some changes, it takes *practice* to unhook the patterns and reactions we have mastered. For others, just adopting a different view, a different way of thinking about what is happening (creating a new wiring template) can cause dramatic changes over a short time.

Let's look at the Law of Opposites (chapter 3, page 52) with regard to the concepts of good and bad (or right and wrong). There can be no good without bad, no right without wrong – by implication if not stated. So, if we focus on telling two-year-old Robin that she is a such a good girl and give her lots of hugs and smiles and tell her she is being good, aren't we pre-loading her with anxiety and fear of ever doing something that we would consider bad? How likely is it she will say or do something that we consider bad or wrong at some point? You can count on it, right? We are aware ourselves of the weight of these expectations of goodness when we say, "I wish Jane and Mary wouldn't think I'm so perfect," or "I wish Danny wouldn't idolize her."

A healthy young child is an experimenter, a boundary pusher, or as Dr. Panskepp says, a "Seeker." And in this process of healthy development, she will think, say, and do, albeit unintentionally, "bad" things – that is, things that we or others consider bad. And we will react. We will, in that moment, in our child's view, withdraw our love and support. While we can attempt to overcome this problem with lots of praise for what our children do, the times we do react are nevertheless easily perceived as threats to love and belonging. We cannot escape this issue using the knowledge and skills we have now. We cannot go beyond what is normal, beyond what is considered "good parenting," unless we can find a way around or through this issue of good and bad. The concepts or ideas of good and bad, like right and wrong, have a persistent way of coloring our messages with a threat to belonging, especially when we are upset and as we use our disciplinary strategies. At the same time, our ideas of good and bad have been and can be useful. We will explore this confounding issue in depth after we explore early learning a little further.

VI. The Magic of Early Learning

*W*hat we see in the crib is the greatest mind that has ever existed, the most powerful learning machine in the universe.

— *Alison Gopnik, Ph.D., et al.*[34]

Trial and Error

In the late eighties and early nineties I was introducing computers into my company's early childhood programs. I would try out new programs at home before installing them on the computers in the centers. One weekend I brought home a Disney program that had Mickey Mouse and his friends doing different activities in various rooms of a house. I booted it up and then as I read cover on the box, I realized I had left not only the instructions but also a color-coded keyboard cover at the child care computer center. This special soft-rubber keyboard cover obscured the standard keyboard symbols with colors and shapes to use to manipulate Mickey's travels and activities. I put the box aside and thought, "Well, I'll check this out next week when I go back to the computer lab." I left the program running on the computer.

---

34 Gopnik, Ph.D., Meltzoff, Ph.D., Kuhl, Ph.D., <u>The Scientist in the Crib</u>, Harper, 2001, p1.

An hour or two later, Auguste, who was 3 at the time, called me over to the computer. "Daddy, look!" she said, and she proceeded to show me all the things Mickey could do and all the places he could go. I watched her push different keys to get Mickey to go different directions to go into different rooms, to pick up and use different objects in the various rooms, change the décor in the rooms, etc. It was quite complex. She had learned which keys to push to make Mickey do whatever she wanted him to do. She had learned the whole program with no instructions and no color-coded keyboard cover. And she had learned it in probably less time than it would have taken me or anyone else to "teach" her, and maybe in less time than it would have taken me to learn it using the instructions.

How did Auguste learn this? Trial and error! Push a button and see what happens. Young children are continually learning in this way by merely sensing – observing, hearing, smelling, touching and sometimes tasting. Then they experiment, make predictions, and test them out. Auguste was not unique in this way – in an hour or so any three-year-old who felt safe to explore the program would have discovered which buttons would cause whichever responses he wanted. Now consider this: if it takes an hour or so for a normal three-year-old to figure how that computer program works, how long would it take your young child to figure out which "buttons" to push to get you to do what he wants? How long did it take your child to learn which parent to ask for something, you or your spouse, to increase his chances of getting a "yes?" How long to figure out when to ask for something and when not to – just by looking at your demeanor in the moment?

The amazing amount and quality of learning that babies do has been sensed and observed by parents (especially mothers) long before there was a science of human behavior. When human behavior became of scientific interest, babies and children became subjects of research and studies. Over time, theories of children's behavior have shifted while ways to teach have not changed significantly.

As of this writing, it has been shown that babies recognize meaning of some spoken words as young as 16 weeks – without having had the "benefit" of any teaching methods.

How do children learn to talk? The answer to this is very revealing about the amazing capacity for learning that young children possess. Learning to talk requires being able to separate sounds coming from adults mouths into discreet "sound bites" that mean something or that connect those discreet bites (bytes?) in a specific way. This means distinguishing one word from another, and discovering what each represents. But, if the research is accurate, babies might be doing this at sixteen weeks!

Have you ever listened to someone speaking in a totally foreign language? Can you tell when one word ends and the next one begins? What if one person has a different accent from another? Our children learn many words by "asking" us – pointing to something as saying, "whah ...?" and we say, "doggy." And whether our child is pointing to a cartoon dog, a photograph of a dog, a real dog, or a hot dog, each has the same sound yet a very different look, smell, and taste (!). For each object, a young child associates the visual data with the sound of the word that is said when the object (or person) is pointed to. And there is more data being associated at the same time. Where is this object located? What does it do? How do adults (parents) relate to it? And more: this time the dog is in the park playing with other dogs, this time mommy says, "don't touch!" And more: this other thing that is smaller is also called a "dog" so suddenly "dog" becomes a category of object (animal, canine, greyhound, female, etc.). There is little difference to the brain whether two or three associations or many more occur – if mommy or daddy pay attention, baby pays attention.

Remember how exciting it was to hear your child's first word? (Ma ma or da da?) You may have noticed they were already understanding much of what you were saying, and in another year you could understand what he or she was saying.

Think about this: how many muscles are involved in saying a word so that another human being can understand it? Diaphragm, throat, vocal chords, lungs, mouth, lips, speed of breath, all are carefully coordinated to say "ma ma." Do you know what the average three-year-old's understanding vocabulary is? If a child's parent has a large vocabulary and talks with her child – conversationally – that child, by three, can understand the meaning of well over 1500 words.

And what about numbers and math? "Babies are born accountants. They can estimate quantities and distinguish between more and less," says Dr. Elizabeth Spelke, a researcher at Harvard University.[35] The implication is that useful number (computational) skills can be learned earlier than we may have thought, depending on our pedagogy for setting up how they might learn them.

Let's then think some more about very young children and learning. What sensory input are they gathering? Everything they experience in the physical world appears to come through at least five "data gathering channels": seeing, hearing, smelling, tasting, and touching. Every sense used, every experience of the object explored, is recorded/absorbed very quickly. You can tell by watching. As soon as a baby has absorbed what there is to absorb from one item, she puts it aside and reaches for something else. Each of those "experiences" or "experiments" causes other associated sensory experiences – links to each of the other senses: very pointy, sharp, pain, for example. Or bendy, thin, hard, "snap!" Or soft, mushy, warm on ear, mommy, smile. The closer in time each sensory experience occurs (meaning milliseconds here), the stronger the link between them.

---

35 Angier, Natalie, "Insights From the Youngest Minds," NYT Profiles in Science, April 30, 2012.

What new objects and concepts in language are our children learning every day? Rocks are hard, bath water is warm, birds tweet, and so does Auntie Joannie! What skills are they developing in their interaction with the world and their ability to get around in it? How best can we support and enhance all of these?

Our children have a built-in developmentally ordered process. Healthy development will happen naturally, on it's own, and in its most effective way, when we provide a supportive environment. This environment includes encouragement, access to the "stuff" of the world, and the opportunity to interact with it. It begins to unfold when we give our babies freedom of movement in safe environments, allowing the most basic interactions with their immediate environment. Putting them on their tummies on a flat, smooth but firm surface, for example, encourages early mobility development such as crawling (salamander-style, on their stomachs), creeping (on hands and knees), and walking, as well as great eye-hand coordination. Climbing structures like overhead ladders develop more eye-hand coordination and upper body strength and coordination. Confining babies and young children for long periods of time in cribs, strollers, and wheeled or springy seats, although convenient and sometimes necessary, inhibits their freedom to move and reduces the time spent in developing their mobility skills.

There are many categories of learning that can provide a useful way to begin to think in general terms about your child's learning and development:

- Fact-gathering about the physical world through use of the senses (seeing, hearing, touching, smelling and tasting) and linking them together as experiences;
- Practical (survival/belonging) information about what is important to retain and what is not;
- Physical competencies – mobility, balance, coordination, strength, stamina;

- Cognitive competencies – conceptual skills, identifying objects, words, quantities, creating and labeling categories (e.g., animals, numbers, automobiles, professions, sciences, etc.), imaginative skills (visualizing, planning, describing, organizing, etc.)
- Communication – language(s), emotions, social skills (listening, inspiring, supporting, cooperating); and
- Contributory (relational) social competencies – integrity, generosity, respect, appreciation.

This is not meant to be an absolute or complete list, but it provides a starting point to give some useful distinctions within this huge arena of learning. Don't worry about which is more important. Virtually all learning is a part of a holistic process: development in any one category increases the potential ability in many others.

A Walking Story

Brynn, our first daughter, began walking one afternoon while we were on vacation in northern Michigan. In the cottage where we stayed, the living room and dining room were not separated by a wall, so one could walk from the side of the living room at the front of the house all the way across it and through the dining room to the sliding glass doors in the back of the house.

At 14 months, Brynn had been pulling herself up and "cruising" for weeks, holding on to the couch. This time she pulled herself up, turned toward the sliding glass doors on the opposite side of the house, and let go of the couch. She balanced herself by holding her arms up and out in front of her, and took a step or two. She then either sat or fell down on her bottom. We watched with great interest, but knew enough to not try to help her or look disappointed. We just smiled. She didn't get up to try again; and crawled over to do something else. The next afternoon, at the exactly the same time, she did the same thing – she pulled herself up using the couch, and started taking steps. She took a few steps this time, before ending up on her bottom on the floor. Again she just crawled away to do something else. The very next day, again at almost the exact same time, she made it almost all the way over to the sliding doors on the other side of the house. And again the next day, the same time, she made it all the way. As soon as she touched the doors, she sat down for second or two, and then crawled away to do something else. We were all thrilled — I'm sure she could see that in our eyes, and she smiled. But none of us tried to get her to do it again. Every day, each afternoon, she would get up by the couch and toddle across the room to the sliding doors, and then crawl away to do something else. We could see her progress each day — slightly more confidence, fewer moments of swaying, and a satisfied sense of accomplishment on her face. She was free to master it herself, and at her own pace, with no apparent pressure or fear of disappointing us.

Don't we parents typically lift our crawling or creeping toddler to her feet, hold her arms, and lead her forward thinking we are helping her to start to learn to walk? This would be like a gymnastics coach telling a student gymnast to skip basic swinging and go right to a double-flip dismount (or whatever it might be called). If the coach is a good one, she would instead look to see if her student looked fluid, graceful, and confident before suggesting that he move to the next level. In like manner, if our child is not yet crawling or creeping with confidence and excellent balance and coordination, we (yes, Big People) can get down on the floor and play crawling games. We could pretend to be salamanders or lizards. We could make nests in the far corners of the house and crawl between them — and have fun doing it!

How many muscles does it take to creep or crawl forward? Thirty? Forty? One hundred? According to the National Association for Child Development, stomach crawling (creeping) engages virtually all of the muscles of the body, from the arches of the feet, to the abdominal muscles, to the neck muscles, all of which are used in the process of moving the body forward across the floor.[36] Crawling is a complex motor skill. Once a child's crawling becomes easy, efficient, and graceful, it also becomes not so interesting and challenging to her. Our child's hindbrain takes over the skill automatically, as it tends to do with everything that is repeated over and over (i.e., with practice). Then the child "seeks" to move on to what is next.

We do not have to tell our child what is next for him in his physical growth and coordination skills – his environment will invite and challenge him, and his actions will tell us. Having exposure to and free time with many different things with which he can interact builds and strengthens his thinking, imagining, balance, coordination, and strength. All this suggests that our job as parents is to keep our focus on the environment we are providing: the physical environment, the emotional environment, the social environment, and the relational environment, each one safe and healthy in its own way.

Trusting your child's innate process of development is one of the most effective and stress-freeing parental strategies I have ever learned, and it applies in every area of learning and development. Children's growth and development will happen without our help. We do have a role to play, however. This role, after being sure our child is safe and healthy, is to celebrate the learning and skills that have been developed, and to keep giving our young children lots of opportunities to use and refine their motor and cognitive skills. For example, we can take them to the park, and have fun with them as we let them "self-direct" their own growth and development. We can trust that they will grow and develop naturally as long as they have safe opportunities and enough time.

---

36 Robert J. Doman Jr. and Ellen R. Doman, Down Syndrome: The Importance of Crawling on the Stomach, NACD Newsletter, National Association for Child Development, October 2009,
    http://nacd.org/newsletter/1009_down_syndrome_crawling.php

By the way, I do not suggest that we always just turn them loose and then sit back and watch. Children love to watch their parents play! And, of course, they really love to have their parents join in, but as players, not teachers or monitors. Athletic and physically strong parents have a very special opportunity with their children. In traditional families this role has been commonly played by dads. Children love to have a parent pick them up and swing them around, and many love to jump on a parent and roll around. This is great activity for vestibular and kinesthetic development (intentional movement and control). Whoever is most drawn towards this, with good judgment and awareness of their child's comfort level, is the best one to do this. Remember, safety and security first, then development. Carolyn and I both worked full-time when kids were growing up, and we frequently shared and shifted responsibilities for taking care of our children and our home, nevertheless I was primarily the one who threw our girls up in the air, and played on the monkey bars and overhead ladders with them.

In my preschool "teaching" activities (providing access, opportunity, and encouragement) I have to admit I never paid much attention to the "ages and stages" handouts after a while. Too frequently I saw parents use them to compare their young children to other parents' children, and then, if their child wasn't as far along, begin to think there was something wrong with either their parenting or their child. Possibly influenced by mirror neurons, but certainly perceivable in some way, a parent cannot hide this kind of feeling or sense from her child. This is a very subtle yet significant message to a young child's hind brain. I learned how to "read" children's emotional and physical learning states to some degree before we had our own girls. I learned to pay attention to their level of strength, balance, confidence, grace, and coordination, and when I could see all of these, I would know they were ready to go the next step in their learning and development. I never said anything about it, I would just look for more challenging activities and projects. And, in my classrooms, I became very aware when there was no observable progress in any specific area for any of the children. You don't need to be an early childhood development expert to be observant and notice as your child develops more and more skills. You will notice, and from time to time your child will "show and tell" you.

If there is no play role-modeling from a parent as a Big People, a child may adopt the view that playing is not important to becoming an adult and belonging in the culture. If the play is too directed by a parent, teacher, or older sibling, or if there is not enough free time to fully explore and experiment with available materials, a child will become frustrated and upset as her need to experiment and explore is not met. This slows development. Think of your own learning: isn't the best, if not the only, way to learn to drive a car accomplished by driving it?

Inadvertent Teaching

When our young child persists in behaving in a way that doesn't work for us, one or more of our usual responses in that specific situation may be working in some way for her, in her internal perception. When this occurs, her behavior has become strategic and is no longer experimental. That doesn't mean she likes it or consciously wants the responses we give to her behavior, such as our yelling at or threatening her or sending her to her room. It might, however, be an attempt to satisfy an innate drive, either for learning or belonging. It could be as simple as "Mommy always takes good care of me when I am upset, so if I get upset a lot, mommy will be happy about being a mommy [she can fulfill her role as care-taker], and will want me to be around." This is one example of something referred to as "child-logic" by some psychologists, and sometimes called "magical thinking." Though it is not necessarily something thought out by the child, it is nevertheless very logical thinking, based on patterns of observed behavior and without our adult filtered lenses. It is consistent with the information very young children have already collected about relationships. Having opportunities for free play, exploration, experimentation, and getting lots of time for repetition of familiar games and stories, has a more valuable long-term impact on our child's behavior.

When our child is ready to move on and doesn't have or see what opportunities or resources she could explore, there will be some behavioral manifestation. Boredom, restlessness, frustration, tantrums and other ways of demanding your attention – these are all possible signs. If your child complains of being bored, that is a good sign that she's ready for some new next step. When my girls came to me and complained, "I'm bored!" I'd say (sincerely), "That's good – that means you might be ready for something new. What do you think? Is there something you could ask for that you aren't asking?" or, "I've got an idea ... why don't you start setting up a circus with the animals and blocks for your dolls to watch? I'll come and take a look when I'm finished with this article." How we respond to our children in these times also makes a big difference in their sense of being loved and supported. They feel it.

When your child is being unusually demanding of you in some way, he may not know why or may not know the words to say. Explore this with him – without expecting that he will know the answer. Just talk about possible reasons, letting him come up with some if he wants to, or suggesting some yourself. Don't assume that you know, however. If you say, "You must be hungry," and then get him something to eat, he learns a strategy for how to get something to eat without asking. If you ask and listen, he will begin to "look" for himself at what he is feeling and thinking. "You know, Billy, you might be hungry, or need a quiet break, or some wild time outside ... I don't know. How do you feel? Do you want something in particular? If you do, feel free to ask me, okay? If it works now, I'll get it for you." Contrast this kind of response from "you need a nap," or "I can't get you anything now," or "you have to learn to wait!"

Healthy growth and development for all people of all ages requires times of activity and quiet times for reflection and rest, allowing a lot of neural integration of the most recent activities with earlier ones. We operate more efficiently when we take time to reflect, relax and let new data (experiences) "percolate." You and I may have a sense of when those times are necessary and how long they should last for ourselves; so too do our children innately "know" for themselves though they may not express it in verbal language. Some annoying and even disruptive behavior may be their attempt to communicate this.

Finally, when a suggestion seems to work, whether your child gets excited about doing something you suggest or tells you she doesn't feel well, that still doesn't mean that was the right or the only answer. We all tend to feel better when someone stops to listen to us, and engages in a conversation with us.

This way of trusting-while-observing your developing child has another very significant impact: your child learns to trust her own body, her own sense, and develops and maintains a natural self-confidence and self-awareness. She picks that up in two ways: first, from your demonstration of your trust and your words of encouragement (the Big People effect); and second, from her own experience of making her own choices and being in her own body. Every skill, every ability, grows with practice. Young children have a natural love of what we adults call "practicing" – until we try to make them practice (because they should, because we're paying for lessons, etc.). For them, when focused and engaged, there is no "practicing." They are just doing what they are doing the way they are doing it in the moment. In their internal process, they are "playing" (exercising autonomy) in the direction of mastery of one or more skills. And the best thing we can do is just to say "you will get better at anything you practice ... it is up to you." This takes the pressure off. Check your List A again and see what is on that list that relates to this discussion.

Children learn by observing us, including making sense of our time observing them. When I managed several large child care centers and was designing staff trainings, I would frequently drive past other preschools and child care centers and observe the staff on the playground. Typically the staff would stand around, mostly near the children, and either watch them or chat, and then jump in when a child did something they weren't supposed to do. And I've watched parents do this on the playground too. Much, if not most, of that it is an automatic "way we're supposed to do it," adopted from our own upbringing and school experience. I recognize that being in a position to see everyone and be attentive to what is happening is necessary when one is responsible for a large number of children in a potentially dangerous place. But as a parent, and as a teacher with an assistant, you can gain a wealth of knowledge about your children when you play with them on a playground and let them take the lead. "But I'm an adult!" you might think. Yes, you are, and you are a Big People. This doesn't mean you always have to play when you take your child to a playground. I am only suggesting that we think about this.

What are other messages might we are giving to children when we assume roles of being monitors or observers? The messages might be: you need to be watched; or we cannot trust you; or it's dangerous here (even when it is not). What are the messages our children take in about adults, particularly about what it means to be teachers and parents? No play? No fun? No excitement, no challenge, no risk?

Studies show that when children (as well as adults) are being observed, their behaviors are inhibited. This may be what is wanted and needed at times, but their cognitive activity (healthy learning and participation) is also inhibited.[37]

---

37 Dutcher, Martin, "Control vs. Choice: The Learning Opportunity in Behavior Management in the Early Childhood Classroom", Early Childhood EXCEL Degree Project, Elizabethtown College, 1991.

Take another look at your List A. What qualities you would like to see in your child? Is there anything about loving her work, or being passionate about her commitments? Wouldn't you love to know your child is enjoying life while accomplishing her goals?

As parents, you and I absorb and react to new as well as familiar experiences in our environment, too. When we don't nurture our own daily growth and developmental periods, we get cranky, we get demanding, we get agitated – just like our children. And who gets cranky first, anyway? It often rubs off, doesn't it? These feelings get translated into associated thoughts, such as "not enough time," "overwhelm," "wishes," "I need a break," or "no one appreciates me." These are messages – to ourselves from ourselves (and to and from our children) – to take some reflective time, or just go out and play. And when there are periods of time in our adult lives when we just can't take the time off to do that, we could ask for support. We could ask someone in our community to look after our children or arrange for them to visit friends, for us to have an evening out to dinner, or a movie, or a quiet evening by the river or lake. That would be good for us and for our children. And what valuable "learning" this would be for our children: adults behave better when they take a break!

The Myth of Motivation

We have grown up in an educational culture that has been misunderstanding children's motivation to learn for over 100 years. Fortunately, this is the easiest part of the book to understand. Here is the big secret: there is nothing you can do to enhance your young child's motivation to learn. Our children are born motivated to learn. It is their focus, their drive. You actually already know this, don't you? It is why our young children exhaust and exasperate us. They never stop! Joseph Chilton Pearce calls this the "model-imperative." In my classrooms, the opportunity to learn something new always got the children's immediate attention.

Daniel Pink, the New York Times best-selling author of <u>Drive: The Surprising Truth About What Motivates Us</u>, cites research, some of which is decades old, that concludes that motivation is created, or increased by, three things: autonomy (choice), an opportunity for mastery (developing valued skills), and purpose (making a difference in the lives of others).[38] What we do in the adult world to attempt to motivate people is use rewards (higher pay and bonuses) and threats (firing or demoting). In schools (on our own children!), we use grades, which carry the risk of shame, embarrassment, and separation. Keeping a child back a grade may cause a great deal of shame and a sense of inadequacy and unfairness. Passing a child who has not kept up with the learning standards does not mean she will do well at the next level either. Either way, she may feel she is a failure, stupid, or inadequate. With regard to cognitive learning and performance, these strategies not only frequently fail to increase motivation, they actually undermine it.

As our children grow older and more aware, they find themselves more frequently in environments where adults determine the agenda: day care, preschools, schools, universities, and jobs. All these environments are concerned about motivating the people within them, and most have adopted old and out-dated methodologies for nurturing motivation. Using strategies that undermine motivation results in our thinking that there is a problem with young people's motivation. The evidence suggests, however, that giving children more choices and relating to them in less controlling ways increases their intrinsic motivation, and thus increases their participation and activity level in learning activities.[39] There is work to be done in our public institutions, and in protecting our early childhood environments from being co-opted with regard to several of these misunderstood factors.

---

38 TedTalks: Daniel Pink on the surprising science of motivation, www.ted.com
39 Dutcher, Martin, "Control vs. Choice: The Learning Opportunity in Behavior Management in the Early Childhood Classroom", Early Childhhod EXCEL Degree Project, Elizabethtown College, 1991.

Are we, as parents, using these outdated and erroneous strategies at home? Do we allow them to be used on our children in their schooling? We do. I did. And our children notice this. It is what we adopted early, what we were taught, and it is the nature of the environment in which most of us lived our first eighteen years or so. It is the way our educational system is set up, and has been for over 100 years. How could we do other than that? Now, by seeing this, we have an opportunity to make a choice going forward, but first we will begin to create an essential tool for having our children thrive in whatever circumstances they will find themselves. Yes, we can, in a sense, "correct" their behavior, give them more useful "data," and question their conclusions without inhibiting their sense of belonging, worthiness, brilliance, and heart. We will need another tool in our toolbox, however, to add to our Big People role, as we increase our awareness of our children's capacity and drive to learn, drive to belong, and accepting our frequent hindbrain interruptions and upsets – including its subtle but strong resistance to being "forced."

VII. Hidden Contexts and Paradigms

*T*he story... *helps us understand that the setting in which we find ourselves affects the kinds of responses we give.*

— Jerome Harste, Ph.D.[40]

The story Harste refers to is one in which a child says what he thinks the answer to a question would be were he not being asked by the pastor of his church. Harste's point for early literacy researchers is that young children's responses are determined by more than acquired factual knowledge. And this then leads us to ask, what else influences our children's responses to our requests and exhortations?

What is a "Context"?

As parents and teachers, like most adults, we tend to think and act as if what we say (the content) is the most significant part of our communicating with our children, and especially when engaged in teaching (whether we are a parent or a teacher).

---

40 Harste, Jerome, & Woodward, Burke, (Indiana University), <u>Language Stories & Literacy Lessons</u>, Heinemann Educational Books, 1984

Here is an example: You are in front of your children and you ask a question, knowing that at least some of them know the answer. Let's say you asked, "What would you like to learn about this year?" No one raises a hand. They stare back at you as if they didn't even hear the question. Why does this happen? Certainly the response (it is useful to consider that the lack of response is a specific response) is not because no one knows an answer. So the problem is not with the question – the content. The lack of response is due to the context. In this example, the context could be pre-existing: the children have been asked this before, and something happened – there was some consequence. Perhaps nothing was done about what they said they wanted and no reason was given, or, more consequential, their answer was turned around and used on them: "I thought you said you were interested in railroad trains – you'll never be able to design one if you don't do your math homework!"

Contexts can also be created in the moment of speaking and acting. The way someone says what they say, and the way in which they do what they do, matters. This "way" I am referring to causes a context to be created. A context can cause predictable reactions, which in turn can reinforce the context. Let's define "context":

> **Context** *n. A perceived intent or meaning of occurrences within a specific environment during a specific time period.*

For example, what a church hall is used for (the intent of the activity), will be different at worship service times than for community project times. How a teacher's personal intent or meaning of his comments will likely be different when she is in the classroom than when she is at a social event with her students.

Adults have various contexts for their interactions with children, and children pick these up. Some parents have a very strong tendency to "teach", expecting their children to remember what they are being taught. Other parents leave the teaching to teachers and may prefer having more frequent purely social and play-type conversations. How a child behaves around each is determined by that adult's context, even more so than the adult's role (teacher, parent, friend).

Think about this. When did you begin to learn that the more an adult knows about you, the more likely that knowledge will be used to control you, to get you to do something – if the adult is a teacher or parent? Isn't this part of the reason you didn't tell your parents about what you were doing after a certain age (not to mention what happens if they get upset)? If this is true, then what could we say about the perceived (not necessarily the actual) context within the classroom or teaching time with a parent? A context of control, one of "getting them to do" something, we now know, causes resistance. No one speaks up, and some try to look as uninterested in anything as possible.

A teacher in this situation can throw up her hands and say, "These kids are just not motivated! They are only interested in the smart phones and texting their friends!" No, they are highly motivated to learn, and highly resistant to being under someone else's control. They are highly interested in being in control of themselves, and that is one attraction of texting: autonomy and secrecy. The other attraction to smart phones is access to learning more about what they are really interested in without upsetting us, the current best solution to The Children's Dilemma.

In a classic Peanuts cartoon, Lucy is complaining: "No one wants to turn my jump rope for me" ... "they all say I'm too crabby. They say I complain too much when they turn it too fast, and when they turn it too slow. No one understands us crabby people." Lucy is right. They think *she* is the problem, rather her context for attempting to get people to turn her rope at the speed she wants. We can see ourselves in this picture, can't we? We know we aren't the problem when we don't get what we want, don't we? And we are right. It is not who we are that causes the problem, it is how we communicate.

Social groups, businesses, churches, schools all have their own contexts. These are intended to be consistent with value or mission statements. Contexts are strongly influenced by, if not determined by, the leaders of the organizations. Some examples of organizational contexts can be "service," "welcoming," "open," "conservative," "kid-friendly," "fun," or "strictly by the rules."

A context can be created or replaced when a leader chooses to do so. Otherwise, when no intentional choice is made, the context will continue to be what it has been in the past, as contexts have momentum. The already existing context is called the default context. You can get an idea of your own default context by recalling what people say about you (or imply by what they won't say about you!). "Nice", "thoughtful", "narrow-minded", "opinionated", "critical", or "hard-driving." These are examples of contexts attached to specific individuals; that is, how their "way of being" is perceived by others.

Contexts not only affect behavior, but also our view of the world and other people. And some, if not most, began early in our lives. The following story illustrates what I mean:

The Sailing Survey

Jackson was my insurance business mentor, friend and colleague for a number of years, and he loved to sail. He had acquired a charter license to sail large sailboats and would take friends out on his sailboat on weekends. He was also African-American. At the office or over lunch we would talk about race and race relations from time to time. He was older than I and raised in the south. One day he was talking about being a black man and sailing out on the Chesapeake Bay. He said that white people don't want to see black people sailing expensive sail-boats on the Chesapeake, and he knew this because of this experience: he would watch oncoming yachts and as they passed by, he counted the number of people (nearly 100% were white) who waved to him. It was about one in ten.

Over the next several months we chatted in some depth about our own experiences with racial feelings and reactions, comforts and discomforts. He remembered the lynching of local black man in his community when he was a child. Our chats were eye-opening for both of us.

A month or two later we took a break from our work and started chat-ting as we did several times each week. He said, "By the way, Marty, I went sailing over the weekend... and I did something differently. Whenever another sailboat approached, I waved to the people on board. Nine out of ten smiled and waved back." His eyes teared up.

This story illustrates the power of context: how the intent and meaning ascribed to the behavior of others can limit our view of people and what is possible. The most significant impact of context on world peace is how an established context – a previously learned intent and meaning – of the behaviors of others keep conflict from resolving. It looks like we get stuck in the past when actually the past context is what is calling the shots, not we ourselves. How can we use contexts? One of your most significant and powerful oppor-tunities as a parent is to be the context creator in your family. Since contexts impact the thinking, the feeling, and the behaviors of people, you can begin creating a context in which exploring, experi-menting, and being loved unconditionally, can co-exist. For example, going back a chapter or two, what context might alleviate some of the dilemma our children have to both explore and experi-ment, and continue to feel loved and supported (the two innate drives your child has no control over)? A context of "it's okay to make mistakes," or "it is okay to say how you feel," are possible starting points. Our children are paying close (but not necessarily conscious) attention to our behavior and expressions with regard to our expectations and responses to them.

Characteristics of Contexts

Contexts, like physical objects, 'behave' according to rules. For example, in order to move or change them, we follow the rules. Physical objects persist on their own. When you stop talking about a tree in the park and talk about something else, the tree itself remains. Contexts, by contrast, exist by virtue of a consistency between our conversational messages and our behavior. When the conversation and behavior regarding a new context stops, the context reverts to the old automatic (default) context. Already existing contexts cannot be erased. But they can be replaced by another context under certain conditions. When a new conversation and behavior remains consistent over time with a new context, the new context becomes established, and, over time, becomes automatic, just as we would expect.

What does it mean to be a context-creator for your family? A context-creator is the one who draws attention to the context present at any time, and then requests and/or demonstrates behavior consistent with it. This is an ideal role for a parent for many reasons. For one, your family is a small enough community that whatever you say and do affects everyone in it directly. If your children are young enough, it is natural for them to say and do what you do. If you have a parenting partner, and you both have aligned on a List A for your family, you have double the impact. If your children are older, they have developed strategies for belonging based on your old default context. It will take time, compassion, and honest communication from you for them to adjust.

What context should you create in your family? There is no should about it. Ask yourself, what context could you now create in your family? Review your List A and make something up. This is a learning process, and you, just like your child, learn best by experimenting. You may find it helpful, at first, to notice contexts "out there," such as in a meeting you are observing or an interaction between a parent and child in a grocery store or playground. Notice all the languages – tones, facial expressions, and body movements – and how they occur for the "actors." Once you can do this, then begin to notice the context in your family at a certain time of day and type of activity, such as dinner time, homework time, or bed time. What has the context been? "Frustrating," "silent," "oppositional," are examples. How does the context get expressed? Sighing, rolling of eyes, stomping around, frowning, curt commands – there are a lot of ways and patterns. What context would you like to replace it? Calmness, respectful, supportive, and/or cooperative are some examples. Our stated context for all staff at Child's Play Learning Centers was the heart of their job description: "To create learning opportunities in an environment of unconditional love, support, and respect."[41] This one statement of context was the basis for virtually all of our staff training, and it makes those centers very special places for children and their parents.

Two examples of common contexts are "work" and "play." These have become important in philosophies of learning, and there are now studies revealing significant advantages of play over work when it comes to learning and accomplishment. But what you and I mean by "work" and by "play" can be significantly different. My "work" was being a staff member in a preschool, while my activity was "play," every day.

Play As a Context for Learning

Many of us today are aware that play is valuable, at least for young children. At the same time, we have been raised in a culture that also values hard work. These two categories of activity are both

---

41 Created by founder and president, Philip N. Adams, Child's Play Learning Centers, Reston, VA.

involved in learning and growing, but in our culture they frequently occur as being at odds with each other, especially in our children's lives. Don't our children (if not our spouses or partners!) quickly choose to play over something that appears to be, feels like, work? Play is a way of experimenting, testing, refining, or performing activities no matter whether they are our "work" activities or our "play" activities. Exploring and experimenting (without fear or judgment) is the safest, most efficient, and satisfying way for human beings to learn new things. Play, especially imaginative play (actually, I'm not sure there is any other kind), has a huge developmental value and thus affects our children's future ability to be successful and accomplished. Here is what Glen Doman, one of the founders of the Institutes for the Achievement of Human Potential, has to say:

> *Imaginative play gives the child the opportunity to exercise his cortical muscle and to experiment with the data. The child naturally wishes to create an effect of some kind. Usually the bigger the effect created the better. When he plays he can see what experiments produce the biggest effect and which ones fall flat. He will certainly store what works and discard what does not. Data that has not been tested is not as easy to retrieve as data that has been tested and found to be useful. This tested data will be stored in the front files and will be much easier to access when he needs it in the future. This means his data bank and processor (the brain) will be more useful to him. He will develop the idea that exploration, discovery and creativity are easy for him and fun. He will seek to do more.*[42]

If imagination, play, and collaboration were designed into our schooling as essential components, as valued as practice and explor-

---

42 Available at the IAHP, www.iahp.org/

ation, what difference would this make in our standing in scientific and mathematical leadership in the world tomorrow?

Having said that, I have another observation that points out something that we frequently misinterpret. When someone is fully engaged in what they are doing, neither the concept of work nor play are present for them. Time flies by. However, an outside observer, noticing their focus and full engagement over an unusual amount of time (in their perception), may say that she "worked hard." We, as parents and teachers, may feel we should tell our children that success comes from hard work, but in doing so, we attempt to force a specific context onto our children's learning activity that can occur as confusing or contradictory to their experience. In addition, children who are already operating at a high level of focus and engagement may end up questioning the value of those moments because their learning isn't occurring to them as "hard." I suggest we use "work" to describe activity we engage in when our focus is on some specific result beyond our enjoyment of the activity itself, such as getting paid or meeting a request for someone else, and "play" to describe an activity we do for enjoyment, or recreation, or for no reason whatsoever. Any kind of activity *can* be done playfully, thought it may not be appropriate for some kinds of activity. One can also be playful as well as serious in any activity, and learning which context causes what to happen is a valuable experimental learning process.

Recognizing the many personal, family, and organization contexts *as contexts* is an extremely valuable social tool, but in attempting to change them we are going to confront another context. It is a huge and very specific context, and thus I call it a *paradigm*. It is so pervasive and old that we don't ever think of any alternative to it. It's roots are in our human history and in our implicit memory, and is then reinforced in our social environments going forward. Being able to see this ancient paradigm in action is the first key in resolving both our parental discipline dilemma as well as The Children's Dilemma. We discuss this in the next chapter.

VIII. Old Paradigm, New Paradigm

I see you looking around at the people in the street;
Life is not what it seems.
If you push them hard enough you will find they do not feel worthy of
love.
How did this come to be?"

— Lyrics by Jane Siberry, "The Gospel
According to Darkness," When I Was
a Boy (album).[43]

An Ancient Behavioral Paradigm

The lines from Jane Siberry's song above reveal a common and enigmatic human condition, perhaps more pervasive than we have realized: a lack of a consistent feeling of being worthy of unconditional love, and that it takes some kind of event ("push them hard enough") for that condition to be acknowledged, as if many of us are pretending that we experience being loved unconditionally. More likely, we have no way of knowing what unconditional love feels like until it happens. Many, perhaps most, of us know or believe that we are loved by our parents, but having that bit of knowledge or belief doesn't make us feel that way. When how we

---

43   www.janesiberry.com, used with permission.

feel is not consistent with our belief system or how we should feel or want to feel, there may be an unseen context or paradigm at play. Here are definitions of "paradigm" that (together) most closely describe the concept as I am using it:

Paradigm *n.*

1. *An example that serves as a model or template.*
2. *A set of concepts, assumptions, or values, that constitutes a way of thinking of or viewing an aspect of our reality.*
3. *A mental framework—an already existing thought pattern or process.*
4. *A way of thinking which can lead to misleading assumptions or predispositions; a prejudice.*
5. *An efficient thought or judgment process which has likely been tested and affirms results of predictions.*

A specific, huge, and ancient behavioral paradigm is the paradigm of Good-Bad/Right-Wrong. This old paradigm underlies nearly all of our social fears. It triggers threat responses in our relationships with other people. Its way of functioning is similar to a context, but a huge one. It is so large and so old that, even though we are impacted by it many times every day, we don't notice it – it is like the air that we breathe. It is the reason we have survived as a species and as individuals. It both helps us belong and separates us from others. It is an enigma at first, and, like our personal contexts, we cannot just erase it. Becoming aware of it's presence in our thinking, feeling, and behavior is the path to disarming it, much like the way we can disarm our automatic upsets by accepting them as normal human behavior. We will start looking at the paradigm by reviewing our experience of getting upset over behavior, whether our own or another's.

Our experience of being upset includes specific sensations, feelings, thoughts, attitudes, and behaviors. The feelings, thoughts, and attitudes that are most frequently present when we are upset include a thought or feeling that the behavior that occurred just before the upset *should have been different* or *should not have happened.* This automatic *should have* or *shouldn't have* feeling/thinking is an indication that we are being influenced by something that is not happening in the moment but that influences the context of the moment. Something is telling us this and we oblige (we don't, as you may recall, decide to get upset before we get upset).[44] This automatic and universal response points to the existence of this very pervasive paradigm of Good-Bad/Right-Wrong.

Take a look at your List B. Most likely your List B is primarily a list of *shoulds* and *should nots* that are a result of something that you didn't make up or decide upon ahead of time. We each have adopted such lists of shoulds and should nots from the past. This past is a result of our own personal early upbringing (from our Big People), very old ideas that have been passed down for generations in our culture (no matter the culture we live within). Sometimes these already-existing "rules" are only slightly different from those of our spouses and partners, and sometimes vastly different. But what is consistent in our thinking about this, and obvious if we look, is that we automatically think that what should happen is good (or right), and what shouldn't happen is bad (or wrong).

This seems so obvious that you might be wondering why I said it. But I ask you, why is this so? Where did this concept of good or bad, and right or wrong, originate? And aren't there times when we aren't even aware of its existence (when we are playing, for example), and times we are overtaken by a concern about it, such as in our parenting or on the job?

---

44 Occasionally a parent might not actually be upset but puts on an act of being upset, thinking that being upset is necessary to handle a "mis"-behavior. Thinking that it is necessary to be upset may be automatic or may be intentional (consciously believed to be necessary).

It is key to note here that this ancient paradigm does not determine which specific behaviors or actions are good or bad, but "tells" us (probably from implicit memory) that most if not all behavior is innately either good or bad. And, of course, a common first reaction to this is "of course a lot of behavior is either good or bad." Am I saying there is no good or bad? No. I am saying that good or bad, and right or wrong, is an automatic, habitual assessment system that gets triggered. Am I saying that all behaviors are thus classified? No, not necessarily. I am saying that we automatically react as if certain behaviors are good or bad, or right or wrong. We get upset with our children when one of our behavioral boundaries is crossed, or when one of our rules is broken (if not the first time, then the second or third). These boundaries are different for different people and under different circumstances, but boundaries originate deep in our past. Is this a good thing or a bad thing? Did you ask yourself this question? Do you already have an opinion? The paradigm itself is what causes you to ask or answer this question – automatically. Noticing what you already think, or noticing not knowing what you already think, is a valuable exercise. Discerning our thoughts and assessments labeled as good or bad as a paradigm can help us get to the root of why we parents and our children all too typically grow apart and what we can do about it.

The Value of the Old Paradigm

We could surmise that the world would be a more dangerous and capricious place if we (human beings) had not adopted the idea of 'good' and 'bad' with at least some local or community agreement as to what is good and what is bad or what is right and what is wrong. This right or wrong "template" has provided social guidelines – rules – for human behavior. Early in our human history there were many "misbehaviors" (now considered minor) that could cause both our personal demise as well as the demise of our family and community. Any movement, any noise, could instantly attract a nearby predator or enemy. Any "offensive" behavior, or the hint of one, could also mean death or severe physical punishment. Our ancestors needed a quick and effective context for survival behavior, a shortcut that would eliminate any "thinking about" what to do in times when an instant action would be life-saving. Which brain is the most survival oriented and quick to response? Our hindbrain. What are the two survival responses? Fight or flight (or hide).[45]

Notice that the Good-Bad/Right-Wrong paradigm is one that "fits" our hindbrain's way of operating (which, you may recall, is not really "thinking"). Everything is "this or that." We don't initially do a lot of "creative" thinking before we react to things as "good" or "bad" – and especially not with regard to "bad" or "wrong." This is a hint of the survival value this context has had. Another hint that this is a social survival issue is that we seem to tolerate exploring or doing bad things more easily if we think no one will find out about them. We behave as if our survival depends on not only our appearing "good" and being "right," but also that our children are being "good" and doing the "right" things. This latter parenting issue reveals our innate drive to belong to our community. We fear being ostracized or thought ill of, and our hindbrain is activated when a potential criticism of our parenting occurs.

The Problem With the Old Paradigm

Let's get back to the relationship between young children and the Big People. When you and I were very young, we discovered that there are potentially serious (from a young child's point of view) consequences for doing things that our parents considered bad or wrong. These consequences (parental upsets with us) were initially and usually a temporary loss of affinity, affection, protection,

---

45 Note that "don't get caught" encompasses both flight and hiding behaviors. "Don't get caught" is a very common, automatic survival strategy for crossing behavioral boundaries in today's world and operates exactly the same way it did when were very young, and we have gotten very good at it.

approval, and/or a sense of being loved, and may have been followed by punishment, isolation, or further evidence that our survival was under (inadvertent) attack. When our parents discovered
that we had done something bad or wrong, we could tell: they got
upset! Remember, one of the driving forces of a human being
(meaning you and I), by nature, is to belong – first to mother, then
to family, and then to community. This driving force operates as a
pre-programmed function of our brain system, and research sup-
ports this. This driving force – to belong, to be loved, and to be
secure in our knowing that we are being cared for, however, bumps
up against another driving force: the drive to explore and experiment, to find out about the world as much as possible and as soon
as possible. This "Children's Dilemma" is still our dilemma, and
though problematic, it is not a "bad" thing.

Remember, when our child gets a strong bad-or-wrong judgmental
parental reaction (upset at some level) because of a behavioral
experiment or an exploration-driven behavior, their hindbrain over-
rides their cortex, and they go into a defensive, protective, and/or a
"seeking belonging" mode. Our strong parental upsets are experienced by our young children as moments of loss of our love and
support. This is a very high threat level, and while their right-hemi-
sphere cortex is "mirroring" the parental upset, the hindbrain
demands actions (strategies) for avoiding these situations. After a
(short) while, our children get some pretty reliable ideas of what we,
their parents, are likely to consider to be bad and wrong: those
things that result in our getting upset. (And we thought we were
teaching them "right" from "wrong"!) Our children will attempt,
with great sincerity, to avoid those behaviors. Nonetheless, they cannot suddenly stop their natural explorative and experimental ("seeking learning") behavior. They will – necessarily – fail again and
again to avoid behaviors that result in our judgement of either them
being bad or wrong, or that their behavior was bad or wrong. Every
time they fail, their relationship with us is threatened. Gradually,
their enthusiasm for exploration can lessen, and their participation

shrinks[46]. Allan Shore, a noted researcher in this field, estimates that the average child gets nine negative (e.g., No!, Don't!, Stop! Bad!) responses every hour.[47] And for children who weren't engaged frequently in social talking with parents:

> **Dr. Todd Risley:** *" ... with very taciturn parents, it was almost the reverse, they only heard they were right about 120,000 [times], and they had heard they were wrong about 250,000 times. In other words, the massive lifetime experience of these kinds of affirmations and prohibitions indicating you're right and you're wrong is ... "*
>
> **David Boulton:** *" ... shaping the thresholds of your entire affect system."*
>
> **Dr. Todd Risley:** *"That's right. It's a lifetime batting average that's hard to overcome with just a little bit of positive experience."[48]*

And yet our children still try to be "good" and then fail again, up to a point. They don't know about their innate drives, they are (acting upon) their innate drives. And then they come to believe that they are bad or insufficient or missing something integral that Big People apparently have (or at least demand of them). Once they adopt this view of themselves, of who they are, they must adopt a strategy for looking good, including hiding what might be seen as bad or wrong. This becomes an automatic behavior and results in being overly-careful, under-expressive, and non-spontaneous to varying degrees. By the way, note that sometimes there are circumstances when each of these "ways of being" may be useful or necessary, but when

---

46 This is not all undesirable, by the way, but at the moment I want us to consider it isn't all desirable, either.

47 From Pearce, Joseph Chilton, <u>Strange Loops and Gestures of Creation</u>, Goldenstone Press (2011), referring to the research of Allan Shore, PhD.

48 From www.childrenofthecode.org/interviews, with Dr. Todd Risley, Professor Emeritus of Psychology, University of Alaska; Co-Author: <u>Meaningful Differences in the Everyday Experience of Young American Children</u>

these patterns have become automatic most of the time, there are huge social and cognitive costs to our children. This frequently unnecessary restraint in learning is essentially amplified over time and thus is costly to society at large. And this is not to mention the cost for some children whose early lives were so unstable and threatening that they adopted (through no fault of their own) aggressive and/or violent responses triggered by their early childhood experiences.

How we originally became so attached to the idea that any specific behavior is good or bad or right or wrong is an interesting question. Philosophers, theologians, and other people who have studied and thought about this for a long time do not agree on what specific behaviors are innately right or wrong, if any. Any answer seems to always be based on the circumstances and, of course, a person's adopted points of view. For our purposes, we are going to focus on the behaviors within our families, as these behaviors are within our range of our ability to create a context in which they occur.

Our children notice, perhaps before we do, that our spouse's idea, or their grandparents' idea, of what is right or wrong is frequently different from ours. We don't usually address this with our young children, probably because we would have to say, "I'm right but daddy (or grandma or ..) is wrong." But now it might be less mystifying that our attempts to teach our children "right and wrong" don't seem to work in an absolute way.

I do not mean to be concluding that everything about living life and making choices is based only on our personal observations, but I am asking you to look at what our children see and hear from us, and what we see and hear from others. Remember that you and I were young children in the same predicament. Children see and feel every discrepancy, every difference, every bit of hypocrisy in the adults around them. Before they learn and feel the need to meet our expectations, there is just "behavior." (It would be really weird to correct a one week old baby for anything, wouldn't it?) But once our love and approval becomes juxtaposed with our expectations of their behavior, resentment and frustration begin to occur. Now perhaps we can begin to see where our frustration and confusion originates, both in our parenting and family relationships, as well as in our professional relationships. It is how our learned expectations occur in the ancient Good-Bad/Right-Wrong paradigm.

Again, I am not saying there is no right and wrong or good and bad. It is extremely important for our children to understand how good and bad and right and wrong function in our society. Virtually all human behavior exists within this context, and there are severe consequences for anyone who does not know about this.

Doesn't it make sense to tell our children that different people have different ideas about what is right and what is wrong, and what is good and what is bad, since that is what they are already observing? And if different people have different ideas, who is right?

Tough Grandmas

Auguste, about three and a half, was being admonished about some behavior at the dinner table one weekend when both of her grandmothers were visiting. As the dinner was put on the table, Auguste made a face that showed she wasn't happy about one of the dishes we having for dinner. That was not an issue for Carolyn or me, it was just a "comment." First, Becky, Carolyn's mom, told Auguste that what she had done "wasn't nice," and then, Lotte, my mom chimed in with "Yes, that's right!" Then Auguste looked down at her plate, and with a furrowed brow said, perhaps inadvertently too loudly: "Tough grandmas!" We couldn't help but laugh, grandmas especially.

Let's talk about older children for a bit. It is common to think that our teenagers' primary concern about getting caught exploring and experimenting (doing things we've told them not to do) is not wanting us to lose privileges or get "grounded." But a recent study reveals it is actually because of something else: rather than loss of privileges or fear of punishment, the deeper overriding fear is of losing any more of our love and support, of further damage to or losing their relationship with us.[49] Thus, we see that even older children encounter the same dilemma. What can we do about this seemingly inherent problem? First, notice that it is inherent in the old Good-Bad/Right-Wrong paradigm. Within that paradigm it is inescapable.

Fortunately we have language. In fact, if we didn't, we would be more like lizards and snakes – all hind brain, no contexts, and no paradigms. But we do have language, and so we can create another huge paradigm, one that can encompass and include the Good-Bad/Right-Wrong one, allowing our history to just be our history, allowing our behavior to be safely examined and shared, and our future to be something new, a future of relating without causing separation, resentment, and retribution.

A New Paradigm

How do we create a new and inclusive paradigm for assessing human behavior without judging the rightness or wrongness, or goodness or badness, of what happens? If we don't have good and bad behavior, and what is right and what is wrong, how will we know what to do? First, let me assure you – good, bad, right, and wrong are not about to go away. That is not the intention, in any case. Let's start with how to create a new paradigm, which, if you recall, is a very large context.

Remember that contexts cannot be erased. Paradigms, especially one as large and old as the Good-Bad/Right-Wrong one, work just

---

49 *Bronson, Po, and Merryman, Ashley, Nurture Shock, 12 (Hatchette Book Group), 2009, p 39.*

like contexts. New ones can be created to replace or contain older ones. We are not going to be getting rid of the Good-Bad/Right-Wrong paradigm, nor are we going to ignore it. To start, it is useful to simply to pay attention to it and watch how it affects us, both as we proceed and afterward. Now let's talk about replacement for a minute.

As an analogy, suppose you wanted to replace the wheels on your car with something superior to wheels. Whatever you choose as a replacement would by necessity have to do what your wheels do – provide a low-friction way that allows your car to move forward, backward, and turn. For wheel replacement to be worth the time, money, and energy, you would want the replacement to improve the function of the wheels or why bother to replace them? A worth-while replacement would also not disrupt the other existing functions of your car; the windshield wipers and the electrical system would still work. So let's look at the old paradigm in this way.

Here are the positives of the Good-Bad/Right-Wrong paradigm – what we would want to retain:

1. It provides norms or guidelines for human behavior, getting most of us at least on the same page with regard to behavior and societal expectations and security.
2. It allows us to make instant decisions due to its "this-or-that" nature – it is hindbrain friendly, and these quick decisions can save us from harm and even death.

Here are the problems caused by the old paradigm:

1. It results in the hiding of potentially useful explorative and experimental behavior (learning) due to past associations and experiences of threat and loss, primarily because it did when we were very young.

2. It results in the reduction of communication of thoughts and feelings which may cause upset, resulting in diminished communication and lack of intimacy between parent and child.

3. The judgment that some other person or some other group is bad or wrong allows us justify gossip, abuse, injustice, and exploitation of them, no matter what the truth is about them.

What if we could replace this Good-Bad/Right-Wrong paradigm with a new paradigm, one that continues to give us the pros of the old one, and eliminates the cons? And what if it retains a this-or-that (Law of Opposites) aspect that allows our hindbrain to continue to function as the emergency protector? What if we could replace this ancient paradigm with one that, rather than discouraging open communication, actually begs for it? And what if the languages of the new paradigm are already familiar but are just usually overshadowed by our reactive, habitual ways of communicating? The next chapter offers a solution to the problems posed by these questions.

IX. The End of Dilemmas

*O*ut beyond ideas of wrongdoing and rightdoing, there is a field. I will meet you there.

– Jellal ed-Din Rumi (Persian poet and philosopher, 1207 – 1273)

We saw that our parenting dilemmas are a direct outcome of our behavior (via our language and associated messages) and the influence of the Good-Bad/Right-Wrong paradigm. Our children do not want us to think they are bad, at least in the early years, and we have taught them that whether they are good or bad is a result of their behavior. We have taught them that they are loved conditionally, conditional on their behavior. And since we cannot get rid of the old paradigm, we could invent one that both encompasses it, maintains its useful functions, and eliminates its problematic functions. Doing this is a matter of choice, and of language. Choice takes courage, and language takes practice.

I propose we consider replacing the Good-Bad/Right-Wrong paradigm with a paradigm called the What Works/What Doesn't Work paradigm. Since we are used to assessing behavior as "good" or "bad," and do so without thinking, we will now look at the specifics of each situation and ask whether a particular behavior either "works" or "doesn't work" – no matter whether we have already decided that what happened was bad or wrong, or good or right, or whether we haven't yet decided. Asking the question, "does the behavior work?" or "does the behavior not work?" under the circumstances, brings the new paradigm to the forefront.

What would using this new paradigm require, and how would this function? And what do I mean by "what works"? I'll answer this last question first, as it is simple: consider that behavior that leads to anything on your List A is 'what works.' Your List A is what is important to you. These are your targets and goals, and, with the new paradigm, it will be easier to keep your focus on those, since they are what is really important to you. Your view of your role in your family will shift from being an enforcer, a teacher, or critic, to one of being an admired mentor and coach, and even a best friend, if desired – if friendship means being open, honest, and truly supportive rather than enabling behaviors that don't work. Taking this view, and practicing implementing it, means the end of both The Children's Dilemma and the Parents' Dilemma.

Here is a brief review of these two dilemmas:

The Children's Dilemma

Our children can choose either to talk freely with us about their explorations, thoughts, and feelings, risking causing us to be upset with them, be worrying about them, and potentially losing our love and acceptance, or not talk with us about them and keep as much hidden as possible. This may avoid conflict but causes an ever-widening gap of intimacy and sense of knowing each other, or even complete separation. We all learned very early that no one wants to have bad children who grow into bad adults, and we could not figure out how to avoid being considered bad as we maintained our autonomy and desire to explore and experiment. Meanwhile, as adults, we think it makes a difference if we tell them that it is their behavior that is bad or wrong, not them. But it doesn't. How do you know who is a good person and who is a bad person? Our three-year-olds have already figured that out, and so did we.

The Parents' Dilemma

If all of our strategies for getting our children to do what we want are a form of force, then all we are doing when we use them is cause resistance to our demands and requests, exacerbating their problem of how to grow and develop while maintaining a close relationship with us.

The new paradigm allows easy, fast, and relation-building paths in dealing with behavior. You will see this as we examine the pros and cons of the new What Works/What Doesn't. Here are the positives:

1. It provides a thoughtful assessment structure for cooperation and behavior that ensure the survival of individuals, groups, and our human species.
2. It is hindbrain friendly: a specific behavior either works or doesn't work, in certain specific ways. With practice, our hindbrain will learn to respond quickly to those things that never work and always work, and hesitate in its response to what sometimes or usually works, and it will still override our cortex to keep us safe from harm in sudden emergencies.
3. It begs for more communication between us: What specifically is working and what is not? Why or why not?
4. It is free from years and years of threatening and fear-laden associations and habitual responses, including but not limited to, abusive or punishing social strategies associated with the words good, bad, right, and wrong.
5. It's use brings people closer together with greater openness and dissolves disempowering self-images and threat-causing characterizations of others.

6. It is consistent with our early desire to make a contribution — to make things work for ourselves and others.

Here are the drawbacks, or potential pitfalls:

1. It is new and different, and thus will seem strange at first. If it didn't seem strange or uncomfortable, it probably wouldn't work.
2. It will take practice (but remember, you have a young partner who has not yet established difficult-to-change habits and attitudes), and you can enroll an expanding community of people who are committed to making practice and further learning available.
3. Being new and both non-physical and non-habitual, it will disappear — unless you practice, make physical reminders (make notes, post-its, etc.), reread the book, and ask for assistance when you get stuck.

I can live with those drawbacks. How about you? It is quite a change from the old Good-Bad/Right-Wrong paradigm. And, as noted, it will take review, practice, support, and collaboration. In fact, it seems it will take all of the social skills we want our children to have anyway, and this is where we can maximize our Big People effect if our children are very young, and maximize learning how to be an effective partner if our children are older. How do we begin? Choose.

Creating the New Paradigm

A new idea is delicate. It can be killed by a sneer or a yawn; it can be stabbed to death by a quip and worried to death by a frown on the right man's brow.

— *Charles Brower, noted advertising executive, copywriter, and author*

We begin to create this new What Works/What Doesn't Work paradigm, also called a "context of workability," by making a personal commitment to it, and then build a support structure for it. We usually want to agree with something before we adopt it, and likely, with new ideas, we usually start by revealing our concerns about it, or disagreeing with it. That is normal — that is our hindbrain just doing its job. But rather than agree or disagree with it, let's go back to the driving analogy. Consider that this is like buying a new car. Take it for a test drive for long enough to get a feel for it. And if something isn't working, ask for assistance — from your family, to start. "How am I doing?" is a great question. No matter what answer you get, just say, "Thanks!" And if it is critical of you, then ask, "What suggestions do you have?" followed by another "Thank you," no matter what they say. And remember, just like driving a new car that is significantly different from your old car, this will feel awkward at first. After all, you are switching from looking in the rear view mirror to looking out the windshield.

Any new idea or concept begins in our thinking, and in our conversations with others. We talk about it, we consider it, we think about it. Intentionally replacing the old Good-Bad/Right-Wrong paradigm begins with noticing what we are thinking, feeling, and have already said. Then we can begin to change to the languages of the new What Works/What Doesn't Work paradigm. Remember our physical (first-learned) languages? These are our facial expressions, eye-contact, tone of voice, and body language (by the way, the words we use, understood or not, are nevertheless being associated with these other languages long before our children begin to talk). Creating a new context – a context of unconditional love – will involve will involve substituting the language (vocabulary) of the new What Works/What Doesn't Work paradigm for the vocabulary of the old Good-Bad/Right-Wrong paradigm, and making our non-verbal languages consistent with it. When we change our existing patterns of communication, we also change our pre-existing context and interrupt the automatic associated behavioral responses from others. It is in these moments that we have an opportunity to create new conversations – and if we do not take advantage of it, no problem: the old default conversations will happen on their own. Fortunately, whenever they do, the opportunity is there to replace them.

Like young children and behavior, we will "regress" from time to time. This is because the old habitual Good-Bad/Right-Wrong paradigm will, by it's very nature, seep back into our language and actions and take over. When it does, we usually are the last to notice. For us, it will appear that the new context is not working rather noticing that we have slid back into the Good-Bad/Right-Wrong paradigm.

This is a slippery slope. Notice whenever the new What Works/What Doesn't Work paradigm becomes the new "good" or "right" paradigm, or that the old Good-Bad/Right-Wrong one becomes the "bad" or "wrong" one. This will creep up on you. It is very helpful to notice when that happens: you will feel bad, unable, unworthy, or as if something or someone is wrong. Then ask, does it work to see when I am in the old Good-Bad/Right-Wrong paradigm? Does it work to notice why I am having those feelings, that it is the paradigm that is interpreting my behavior, not me (or anyone else)? There is no right or wrong answer to that question. It is about what you want.

You will begin to notice that "it works" also to pay attention to being upset. Be mindful. Consider that there is nothing bad, wrong, or insufficient in what we notice and reflect upon.[50] Doing this frequently is neurologically important for integrating new and old experience, developing new thinking, and learning to apply new and creative ideas. Keep reminding yourself and your family that being upset only means we are human. Telling our child that we are upset when we are upset works. No blame is necessary, on anyone. No shame, on anyone. Nothing is wrong. Upsets get triggered, and you may notice that there are times when you intentionally aim at someone else (usually your partner!) and "pull the trigger." Does that work to get what you want on your List A? You already know it works to get attention ... if that is the kind you want. But for us, as well as for our children, when we do not get the kind of attention our relationship requires, we'll take any kind. Being in a relationship that is unsatisfying or even abusive can be perceived by our need-to-belong drive as better than not belonging at all.

You may now be thinking, "My kids already know when I'm upset ... I don't have to tell them!" If the goal were only for your children to know when you are upset, I would agree. But the goal here is for you to choose what result you want next. Your children will learn either how or how not to deal with you when you are upset. And that depends on what it means to them when you get upset. Does it mean to them that they are a burden or a disappointment to you? Are they an annoyance or a problem to or for you? What do they see on your face and in your tone of voice? All those messages are automatically generated by the Good-Bad/Right-Wrong paradigm when you are upset, not by your conscious or desired intentions. And what the messages mean to your children now was determined by the Big People effect when you were a child – what they meant to you when you were very young. How would

---

50 Or are "mindful of," "present to," "in the moment," "in the now," "reflecting on" (synonymous).

our children learn otherwise? We tell them as we show them. We share our current view of the nature of being human with them.

To update an old and already-learned view, we first allow any upset, ours or theirs, to exist and not make it mean there is any intention to be disrespectful or unappreciative or withhold our love and support. An upset is merely a temporary interruption (a hindbrain intrusion) in our ability to express our love and support. As soon as we are able, as the leader in our family, we begin expressing our love, support, and appreciation newly. After we do that on a regular basis, our child then learns about the nature of an upset. She learns how to deal with her own and those of others. Wouldn't it be satisfying for you to know that is what your child is learning from you every time someone in your family gets upset? (She's learning from you anyway, remember? The question is not "if" but "what.")

For us parents, there is one last, and lasting, problem caused by the old Good-Bad/Right-Wrong paradigm, and it is this: whenever we think that others, especially people we love and admire, might consider that something that we did was bad or wrong, our first and automatic impulse will be to hide that we did it. This is the only solution to the Children's Dilemma – in the old Good-Bad/Right-Wrong paradigm. Having been children, we have learned and practiced our own strategies for hiding our behavior and thinking for many years. According to some research, it takes 10,000 hours of practice to master anything – but you already know how good you got at this with your parents by 12 or 13, yes? Whenever any belonging or support might be threatened, our strong tendency to hide what it was we did or thought, is not because of any personal flaw or shortcoming, but because it is an old and formerly frequently needed human survival skill. By the time we are adults, it has become so automatic that we don't even think about it. The problem, by the way, is not that we hide certain things. Hiding (not revealing) certain things from certain people works from time to time, depending on our circumstances. The problem is that we learned it early and do it automatically without thinking, without noticing. We have no alternative response when we have no awareness of what we are doing.

What did I learn as a parent with regard to this? In the new paradigm my children feel free to talk about whatever I feel free to talk about and am open to hearing. This expands when I talk with them about something I have previously avoided. And there are a lot of learning opportunities that come out of conversations about behaviors that don't work in life as well. The following story is an example of how a parent can turn "bad behavior" (criminal!) into a relationship-building social learning event.

My Daughter, the Candy Store Robber

There was a small independent drug store around the corner from where we lived in the Adams Morgan neighborhood in Washington, DC. One day Brynn (about four at the time) and I went to pick up a prescription for Carolyn. As I was paying for it, Brynn asked if she could have some candy. She was standing in front of the candy counter. I said, "No, not this time." We left and walked home. As we walked in the front door, I noticed she took something out of her coat pocket. Then she noticed I was looking and put her hand behind her back. I asked, "Brynn, do you have something from the store in your hand?" I could see she was hiding something and trying not to show it. I got down at eye level with her, checked my "context" (added a twinkle in my eye), and then I added, "If you do, sweetie, it's okay if you tell me..." I waited. She slowly brought her hand around in front. I saw the piece of candy. As I was noticing my reaction, I could also see that she was feeling bad or embarrassed and was watching my reaction closely. I paused, and then saw an opportunity.

"Did I pay for that?" I asked, as if it might be possible that I did and didn't know it.

"No," she said.

"Oh, then I'm not losing my memory. Did you pay for it?"

"No," she said.

"Oh," I said. "So you took it from the store?"

"Uh-huh... ," she said, reluctantly.

"Let's go clean this up, okay?" I said.

"I don't want to," she said, and almost broke into tears.

"It will be fine, Brynn," I said, "really it will." We walked hand-in-hand back out to the street.

On the way back to the store I told her how stores work: that the own-ers have to buy all the things that they have in their stores from someone else – they don't make birthday cards and candy and medicine. Then we pay them for what we want and they use that money to buy food for their families and to buy more things to sell in their store.

"So," I concluded, "the owner will probably be happy for you to give back the candy."

"Uh," she said grunted unenthusiastically.

"We'll see," I said, dispassionately. We walked in – I was holding her hand – and we walked up to the counter with her in front of me. Her head barely cleared the top of the counter. The man at the cash register glanced down at her and then looked at me. I stooped down next to Brynn and said, "Brynn?" He then looked at her, and she said, in a barely audible voice, "I took this" and she put the candy on the counter. "I'm sorry," she said.

He looked at her, and with a warm smile said, "That was very nice of you to bring it back... thank you," and he smiled at her and then me. And we walked out together.

"You did a great job, Brynn!" She lightened up, and she could tell I was proud of her, as I really was.

Note that even at her age, and in our family environment, Brynn's response to my discovery of the candy was to hide it. The effect of the Good-Bad/Right-Wrong paradigm permeates our culture and our families. Drawing attention to it when it appears is easy: the paradigm whispers in our ear, "something or someone is bad or wrong." We catch ourselves in it at some point. Then, when we ask our child if he feels like he did something wrong, we can be responsible for it: we tell him that he did not do anything bad or wrong, and that he probably learned to feel that way from the way we used to talk to him (or told him). We ask ourselves, what did or didn't work about the behavior, and then we are in the new paradigm.

Addressing the behavior from the new What Works/What Doesn't paradigm unhooks it. In the story, Brynn's experience of her behavior shifted from bad behavior to behavior that doesn't work; my tone, words, and body language kept saying that to her. It took a little while before she was sure I wasn't upset about that, and then the whole thing became an opportunity. Brynn learned about how businesses work, how to be responsible for behavior that doesn't work, that her dad offered a safe place to her to learn when she does something that doesn't work (enhancing a long-term relationship), and that even a four-year-old can apologize to an unfamiliar adult, perhaps causing a shift in a storeowner's opinion of young children.

What could your family life be like in five years if your child began noticing both the new and the old paradigm? What if she began to look through the lens of workability instead of what is good or bad or right or wrong at age three or even earlier? What about when she becomes a teenager?

In the old paradigm we frequently decided whether behavior was good or bad by an initial feeling, even if later we reassessed that. I was initially surprised that Brynn had taken the candy bar, and I noticed a quick "that's wrong!" reaction internally and that my "good parent" identity was at risk. But I had learned a reaction is a flag, a reminder for me. And even if I had yelled at her, looked disappointed in her, or made her feel like she was bad, I could have addressed that as my reaction, and tell her that it does not mean she did anything wrong, and that I love her just as much. Once she experiences that, then the learning opportunities can begin (in the story, before going back to the store).

Your automatic responses are not going to suddenly stop, and everyone will be happy and cooperative. The Good-Bad/Right-Wrong paradigm does not disappear. In fact, it is its presence that helps create its replacement: when something doesn't work, a human brain searches for an alternative; a hindbrain looks in the past (frequently no help there), and a cortex looks in the present, towards the future – if asked. Asking "what works" activates the cortex and acknowledges the hindbrain protection (the bouncer, as you will). Notice that I did not tell Brynn that she did the right thing or a good thing by going back to the store, as that is more of the same old Good-Bad/Right-Wrong paradigm. I just pointed out what worked about it, and then, "Great job!" to acknowledge what she did. If your child thinks that you want her to be good, it sets her up to fear that you will find she made a mistake, and she is back in the Children's Dilemma.

Remember how we know when a behavior works or doesn't work? Read through your List A – What You Really Want Out of Your Parenting. When a behavior is an example of or leads to something on your List A, we could say "it works" rather than "it's good." If it doesn't lead to something on it, we could say "it doesn't work" instead of it is "bad" or "wrong." But to do this it works for you to have available and be familiar with what is on your List A. Your young children will naturally get to know the list over time.

Aren't we just talking semantics here? Yes, and no, so far. The words comprising the language of the Good-Bad/Right-Wrong paradigm, more so than most other words, not only have meanings (semantics), but strong emotional content (associations), all from the past. This makes semantics suddenly very important, especially in parenting.

As we avoid those old associations, including shame, replacing the words and our non-verbal communication with new vocabulary and physical cues, we lay a new foundation for communication for being related. This kind of communication creates a basis for our children to begin to know themselves as able to relate on a full spectrum: love, fear, excitement, disappointment, surprise, etc. They will become perceivers and creators of communication rather than victims of it. This opens up many opportunities for them to lead, to support, to inspire, and to be responsible. Being human, they are still susceptible to fear, approval/disapproval – all the affects of the Good-Bad/Right-Wrong paradigm, but the grip of the fear and the concern for being loved is loosened. Our children will know that they are loved, that it is okay to change their behavior, and nothing and no one is bad or wrong – no matter the responses they get from others. And this will be true for you first, as you begin using the new What Works/What Doesn't Work paradigm.

The following charts show the most common languages of the two paradigms. I suggest first focusing on Chart 1, our non-verbal (physical) languages. They are hindbrain oriented and we usually are the least aware of them. You may recognize what highly paid coaches teach to high performance athletes and business leaders:

Chart 1: Non-Verbal Language of the Paradigms

Right-Wrong/Good-Bad paradigm	What Works/What Doesn't Work paradigm
Standing over/looking down on	Getting on eye-level
Frowning, pursing our lips	Smiling
Using a sudden loud or harsh tone	Using a low, warm tone or a clear, dispassionate tone
Looking away from	Making eye contact
Moving away or turning away	Opening towards (inviting close-ness)
Sighing loudly	
Furrowing our eyebrows	
Raising one eyebrow	
Grabbing an arm, slapping a hand	Any action require to stop from danger or harm; when danger and any upset is over, explain your job

when we change our physical expression, we change our emotional context. When we change our context from one of fear and domination, for example, and instead show surprise and interest in our eyes and gestures, all behavior in our vicinity changes. Noticing how we are expressing ourselves contextually, and the impact that has on those around us, is a valuable and overlooked social skill.

Chart 2: Verbal Language of the Paradigms

Right-Wrong/Good-Bad paradigm	What Works/What Doesn't Work paradigm
is good, bad, right, wrong	works, doesn't work... your choice
should, shouldn't	
must, must not	
have to, don't have to	
need to, don't need to	
better, worse, not as good as	
you are, or what you did, was bad, wrong, good, right	You are great, I love you no matter what. And great people sometimes do what doesn't work.

Read through the two charts on this and the previous page. Make the faces and body gestures, and say the words for each one. (Hey, the sooner you start on this, the sooner it will become second nature to you!)

These two charts contain your keys for opening up or closing down communication with your child under virtually all circumstances. What if it is an emergency, or you are in a hurry, you might ask? It is likely you will use the language of Right-Wrong/Good-Bad, as it frequently works best to shut down communication and take action during an emergency. And probably you and I would make that kind of decision without thinking first – a good thing in this case. We do need our hindbrain, remember.

How does what we have learned about the Good-Bad/Right-Wrong paradigm and what we are beginning to create within the Works/Doesn't Work paradigm, relate to the strategies we have adopted? In the following section we will examine each of the categories of strategies and look for what works and what doesn't work about them. It is then your choice. Each time you choose the languages of the What Works/What Doesn't Work paradigm (creating a "context for workability"), your brain will create and strengthen neuronal links to this new language and new ways of relating to your child's behavior, and new results will be produced. At the same time, your child begins to relate to her own behaviors in the same way you are learning to do that. For both of you, behaviors that "don't work" become opportunities to contribute, and acknowledging behaviors that "do work" become authentic expressions of appreciation and love rather than a "should do" expectation.

Interestingly, you cannot make this paradigm shift incorrectly, do it badly, or wrong. You can only do it or not do it. When you create the new paradigm by simply asking the question, "What doesn't work about this?" something shifts from being a problem to being an opportunity. Your state of mind shifts from a sense of something being wrong or bad (this sense is sometimes so familiar it goes unnoticed) to a sense of opening, and may include some confusion or uncertainty. This is why grounding yourself in your List A works. Your cortex will take over. The shift in paradigm can be very subtle and yet can cause a huge shift in behavior "for no apparent reason" – both your own as well as the behavior of others around you.

This Workshop Isn't Working

One parent, Julie, at the beginning of a workshop said she wanted to feel more appreciated by her teenage daughter. When I asked her to give me an example of what was happening, she said, "Well, usually, when we finish eating dinner, she gets up from the table and goes to her room. This is because she would complain about something I did or didn't do, be very negative, and we would always have a huge fight."

After we distinguished the paradigms in the workshop, I asked the parents to try out the languages of the new paradigm during the week. When we met the following week I asked the parents how it went. Julie said she just wanted to "get on with the workshop." She said she didn't think she'd learned anything. Then I asked, "Was there any change in anything at home this past week?" Julie thought for a moment and then said, "Well, Wednesday evening, after dinner, my daughter Julie stayed in the kitchen and just started talking with me while I was cleaning. up. There was no arguing or complaining. We talked together for 30 minutes or longer. She never does that!"

This mom didn't notice doing anything differently – but her way of being was slightly different. Her non-verbal communication had shifted just enough to allow her daughter's innate but unspoken desire for their relationship to be expressed. The mom's paradigm had shifted, and therefore so did the behavior of both mom and daughter.

By age two or three, our young children have already learned to respond to the old Good-Bad/Right-Wrong context with fear, guilt, and/or shame. I saw it with the preschool children in my class when a parent was correcting or complaining about a behavior. You can see it in their eyes, face, bodies, and attitudes. They will look guilty: avoid eye contact, hang their heads, and either avoid physical contact or seek it to be reassured. They may cry or yell at you, seeking some way to get your love and support in the moment. Our children have learned this response from us via the Big People phenomenon, and we reinforce it as they grow older. Ironically, this is not bad news. We might feel bad or guilty for doing this, but remember that when you were young, you had Big People too. You couldn't help but absorb and model this way of dealing with upsetting behaviors. But now, rather than continue to reinforce this, you can undo it. First, notice when your child is feeling guilty or bad. Then ask about it. Even very young children (with verbal language) will tell you when they feel like they've been bad. Your job is to keep communicating your love until you see and feel your child returning your expression of love in a way that moves you.

Fortunately, our young children will pick up the new paradigm fairly quickly because of the Big People affect. If you are working with older children, it will take longer – they have to learn to trust that you mean what you say. This means telling them when you have been thinking that they have done something wrong or bad. Then find your own way to say, "but I know you didn't, but it sure didn't work!" And then you have something to talk about that *is* useful. We will give some examples of conversations that will work in later chapters. In the meantime, you can look for appropriate times to connect. In the new paradigm, you can be honest. You can talk with your older children about issues you have with them, and where those issues came from. Some are likely to be from your own early life, and some will be from their more recent behavior and behavioral strategies. You and your child will begin to see that your motivation for your responses, whether they worked or not, is your love and your concern for their well-being.

What if your own fear of damaging your relationship with your son or daughter keeps you from being honest and open? I suggest that you find a private place and time, and ask your child for permission talk together privately. Tell him that you have a concern and don't know what to do about it. Then, say why you were reluctant to say what you are going to say. Pause. Then say what you have to say directly to him or her. When you have said it, stop and listen. Your children are more likely to reassure you than you would think – when you are open, honest, and and aren't trying to change them. To love someone is to accept them, just as they are now, and just as they could become. Remember, unexpected change is also a trigger for the hind brain, and you can use your cortex to prepare both your own hindbrain as well as your child's hindbrain for future changes, modifying (and defusing) existing expectations.

The following story is another example of how the way we deal with our children's mistakes, accidents, and unworkable behavior can turn a potentially relationship-diminishing and panic situation into a respected, appreciated, and effective response. A good friend and father of three adult children and I were discussing language, context, behavior, and upsets. He shared an incident with me that he and one of his now-adult daughters discussed not long ago over dinner. Here is his description of the recent conversation:

The Spilled Milk

My daughter, now in her mid-twenties, has always been a perfectionist, and we've talked about that together over the years. The other day she was recalling, from her childhood, that one evening – she must have been five or six – we were at the dinner table and she knocked over her glass of milk. She said she recalled that she had a moment of fear and looked across the table at me. At that time I realized that she was looking for my reaction, and so I looked her right in her eyes, warmly, and said, "Here are some napkins, honey," as I handed mine and an extra one to her. I also begin using one to soak up the milk. She went and got a few more, and we cleaned it up together.

After she recalled the incident, she said she so appreciated the way I reacted. She attributes her own quick yet calm manner of appropriately dealing with "accidents" in her life now to my response way back then.

What if he had reacted with frustration and anger or some other form of upset over the spilled milk? He would have then had an opportunity for two valuable learning opportunities, and the first one is the point I hope you are getting clear about: we automatically react emotionally, however we do. Our job is not to stop reacting. Our job is to observe the reaction as a reaction, and see that it is a way human beings work – literally. And whenever we withhold our love and affection due to being upset, we then talk about it with our child or spouse so they begin to also see that our being upset does not mean that anything is wrong – even though the context around us will likely feel that something is definitely wrong. That feeling, and the thinking that goes along with it, are just as automatic as the original upset. Our new context of workability allows us to let go of the sense of "truth" that something or someone is bad or wrong. The more we practice noticing when we are upset, the sooner we will be able to interrupt it, and even defuse it ahead of time.

Anything you do only because you should do it will not likely be fulfilling, though it may be necessary. If what you are doing or going to do is necessary, then there must be something that works about your doing it. Find that. And that is what to share with your children when they ask or don't understand why you do what you do. Then you will feel fulfilled, and your children will have both a new and supportable understanding of you and how the world works.

Sometimes we find that, especially once we begin to experiment in the What Works/What Doesn't Work paradigm, actions we thought were necessary, may not be. Some problems disappear in the process of examining them, and some occur as learning opportunities that we wouldn't want to eliminate. Example: When your child decides not to do her homework, what outcome goal on your List A does not get strengthened if you continually "make her" do her homework? If your child hasn't yet started school, what could your child learn early in life if you let him be responsible for those things (that he can do himself) without your judgmental commentary and attempts to force it?

X. Re-Thinking Our Discipline Strategies

"And what do you do, Marty?"

"I teach three-to-five-year-olds at Amazing Life Games Preschool."

"Oh, how wonderful. The children are lucky to have a male. You must be so patient!"

"Actually, I am very impatient when young children's behavior doesn't work for them, but they don't notice my impatience."

How do we deal with a persistent behavior that doesn't work? Do we have to put up with it? Do we just talk about it? That doesn't work. We do get to say what behaviors are allowed and what behaviors are not – it is our family, and we, as parents, are accountable. Just saying what is allowed and what is not, however, doesn't provide much of a learning opportunity. Neither does using a behavior management strategy from our parenting manual, List C. But our children do learn from experience, and they have learned a lot about us by age three. What has been our child's experience of us to date? Here are some questions to ponder:

Do we attempt to get them, to make them, do what we want? Yes. Our List C is our evidence. Is that bad or wrong? No. It is only what we learned and have done to date, at least a lot of the time. But we don't tell them that is what we are trying to do, do we?

Do we always, or even mostly, do what we tell them that we will do? Or do we often have good reasons to not do what we say? It depends, and they know what it depends on.

Do we let them know what we are trying to accomplish in our own lives and *why that is important to us* in life? Do you think that would help them understand us – and life – a bit more?

Do you enjoy being with your child? When, and when not?

Does your child have to wait for you to get upset to find out when you aren't enjoying being together? Do you have to have a special occasion (e.g., birthday, graduation) in order to be comfortable telling them how much you enjoy being with them?

Do you see that we adults do not easily communicate things that are important to us? Could that be because it is a habitual pattern we learned as we were growing up, to avoid upsetting our parents?

I never enjoyed teaching children how to behave, neither my own nor my preschoolers. But I noticed that I didn't have to as everyone else was already doing that. I just told them when their behavior wasn't working for me, and why. I brought my own toys to preschool to role-model sharing as well as not sharing, from a "workability" context. (As for not sharing, I refused to share with any child who showed that he might break my toys, or who would not give them back when I asked. That most parents would not share their personal belongings with their peers under the same cir-cumstances, but will insist that their children do it, seems to escape us).

150

The Problem with Strategies

Pulling the Plug on Parenting Strategies
by Auguste Dutcher

The longer I've worked on this parenting project with my dad, the more I've realized how difficult it is to examine my own childhood through the lens of parenting. Like any kid, I always thought that how my family interacted was completely ordinary—even valuable distinctions never stood out at the time because they were woven into the fabric of our day-to-day living.

Here is just one of the awesome gifts my parents have given to both me and my sister. Even as young children, my parents related to us as respected contributors. My dad and I had conversations about automatic feelings and making our family work – really, it was the stuff of parenting. I remember that in my early elementary school years, we would even discuss classroom dynamics and behavior issues on our long car rides to and from the school he managed. He says that this kind of communication started at day one (I'll take his word for it), but in reality I don't remember having a lot of these conversations, at least not anymore. Even editing my own contributions to this book a few years after I first wrote them, these memories don't seem as clear as they must have been at one time.

But the proof that it all happened is that in reading over the distinctions in these pages, most of the concepts seem like common sense to me. I know this reaction stems from the fact that my family was practicing these distinctions long before Dad put them to paper. It's no secret that both parents and children are pros at using strategies to try to get what they want. The difference in our family was that we talked about it, and my sister and I have done so from a very young age. Despite the "grown-up" nature of these conversations, I never remember feeling con-

fused about what we talked about. And I was never told I was too young to understand.

If you consider it logically, you would probably never want to share any of the strategies you use on your children with them. If, for example, you told your children that you yelled at them because you were trying to scare them into doing what you want, yelling would no longer really be an effective strategy, would it? The power would be gone. But that's exactly what my parents did. They still got angry sometimes, and they still acted disappointed sometimes, but most of the time they talked with me about it afterward.

The last point I want to make about disciplinary strategies is this: what is it like for you when you feel like someone is attempting to get you to do something you don't want to do at the time? If they don't stop when you say, "No thanks, please stop asking (begging, offering, threatening) me!", don't you want to just run away? Our children don't (frequently) run away – the belonging drive is far too strong – but they will pull away, little by little over the years..

So let's examine our most taken-for-granted historical behavior modification strategies, starting with the most common, and possibly oldest one. Re-thinking these now will be a useful exercise is seeing what works and what doesn't work about them.

Punishments, Rewards, and Consequences

Punishments

> **Punishment** *n. The pain, confinement, or penalty inflicted by an authority for a crime or fault in order to cause a change in another's behavior.*

By definition there is an implied purpose or agenda to a punishment: to cause a change in someone else's behavior. It clearly exists in the Good-Bad/Right-Wrong paradigm: "for a crime or fault" (something bad or wrong). Furthermore it is typically administered with force-based language (tone, facial expression, and the Good-Bad/Right-Wrong language) and thus naturally causes both a break in relatedness as well as resistance. The most common behavioral result of using punishment is for the offender to learn how to keep from getting caught, while the offender's strategic reason or innate drive for the behavior itself is still operative. Studies show that punishment just doesn't work – it may cause a temporary change, but not a lasting one – with one exception. A child who is raised in an environment of continual punishment does not have an opportunity to learn how to choose behavior. That child can become dependent on having people around her who use punishment as a way of keeping her feeling secure at some level, and not out-of-control.

Rewards

> **Reward** *n. Reinforcement; an act promised and performed to gain and keep approved behavior; something given in return for good or, sometimes, evil, or for service or merit*

We typically have learned to use rewards to motivate our children. Behavioral psychologists distinguish between extrinsic motivation and intrinsic motivation. Extrinsic means external. Extrinsic motivation is a reward someone else gives us because we did something desirable or did something well (to please them or from their point of view). Intrinsic means internal. Intrinsic motivation is what we experience internally – something unique and of value to us personally, and not dependent on outside approval or reward. Personal (intrinsic) satisfaction occurs when children are allowed time for free exploration and experimentation of their own choosing, and when they have opportunities to use and/or play with and use what they've learned. They are more relaxed and at peace, and are motivated to keep learning via exploration and experimentation. As you have likely heard, learning is its own reward.

There is both research as well as anecdotal evidence that rewards do not have a lasting impact of behavior, and that they even have a long-term negative impact.[51] Remember our discussion on motivation?[52] The research tells us that extrinsic motivation is short term, and in the long term it is actually counterproductive (though sometimes a short-term, reward-based reason to change a specific behavior is all that is needed for a child to break a pattern). I propose the following reasons as to why rewarding children does not work long-term: extrinsic motivation (reward) displaces the experience, and thus the development, of intrinsic motivation. Without the intrinsic satisfaction of exploring to satisfy their own personal interests, there is little or no sense of intrinsic appreciation and mastery for children. There is "nothing in it" for them.

Our parental reliance on rewards to motivate our children results in the development of behaviors to gain our approval and a reward rather than their choosing behaviors that make a broader impact, a key requirement for intrinsic motivation. The total message, especially coming from a Big People (and any authority figure later in life), is not merely "do this and we will give you that", but that "getting rewards is the reason to do things."

But children love rewards, don't they? Me too! I am not saying you should not ever give a reward, but instead of using a reward as a strategy to motivate, give one as an expression of your pride or pleasure in seeing them accomplish something. They kept going when they could have easily been discouraged and quit. Also, there is another way to enjoy "rewarding" our children, and that really

---

51 Dutcher, Martin, "Control vs. Choice: The Learning Opportunity in Behavior Management in the Early Childhood Classroom", Early Childhhod EXCEL Degree Project, Elizabethtown College, 1991.

52 Pink, Daniel, TedTalks video, "The Surprising Truth About What Motivates Us"

gets a brain's attention: Surprise! Give them something unexpectedly (that they would want!). This gives you many more options, including allowing you more spontaneity. In short, rewards interfere with self-motivation. Raising children who are self-motivated, creative, and recognize their own passion – these are likely on your List A. Take a look. If not, would you want them there?

Consequences

> **Consequence** *n. That which follows from a preceding action.*

This is a very simple but broad definition. All consequences are potentially valuable (useful or potentially dangerous) for a human being. In our parenting, we use consequences as a strategy to attempt to get our child to change her behavior. And in the existing paradigm of Good-Bad/Right-Wrong, wherein behavior is judged good, or bad, or wrong (where *mis*behavior lives), our parent-given consequences are really punishments: penalties (undesirable consequences) given in order to cause a change in another's behavior.

Let's look a little deeper at different kinds of consequences.

Consequences That Have No Agenda

These are sometimes called "natural" consequences, and in the world of physical laws they are natural – as in the case of gravity. These are pure data-type learning experiences. From these our child will learn which behaviors in which circumstances cause results that are predictable, and which cause random or partially random results. She will also learn, perhaps as early as two, that the non-human world of consequences does not care about her choices – that there is no relational cost to any choice with regard to that world. She will get neither protection from the natural world, nor punishment (intent to change behavior). Gravity has no agenda for any specific human being.[53]

Consequences With an Agenda

When a parent determines and delivers consequences for a child's behavior, there is definitely an agenda: change your behavior – it is bad or wrong – or else! So the consequence itself is designed to be undesirable in order to change future behavioral choices. But another undesirable consequence usually comes along on the ride due to the languages of the Good-Bad/Right-Wrong paradigm: an upset, a threat of or actual separation, a break in belonging, and/or a withholding of love and support. For a child, this may be a temporary condition (for most but not all), but it happens frequently, as we saw when we examined the nature and source of our parental upsets. And in society at large, an arrest, trial, and/or a conviction can and frequently does have a lifetime impact on choices available to secure belonging. The usual, and automatic, effect of human-generated behavioral consequences causes a sense of separation, a threat to belonging, which may have been a factor in the cause of the initial punishable behavior in the first place. The problem for society is, of course, that if a child doesn't learn at least a modicum of social skills by a certain age, she can become a danger to others. And we see that all too often.

Context matters. A parent designed and delivered consequence, when set up and delivered elegantly in the What Works/What Doesn't Work paradigm, doesn't occur as a punishment – not to the child nor to her parent. This specific kind of human-designed consequence (one that doesn't include messages of bad or wrong), is

---

53 Pain, by the way, is usually associated with punishment or that something is wrong (such as in The Skinned Knee story), though when the universe causes pain, or when pain is a consequence of chosen behavior (my daughter's track team T-shirt – "Pain is Inevitable, Suffering is Optional"), pain is can be valuable and/or acceptable. It is not typically so when human beings cause undesired pain for others.

not an attempt to make a child choose A over B because of a threat of loss of parental love and support. And we, as parents, are in the perfect role to create new and non-threatening contexts for behavioral choices within our families. Here are the reasons why we parents can easily create the new What Works/What Doesn't Work paradigm:

- The Big People effect
- The capacity and innate desire for learning "what works" by young children
- The limited impact of young children's mistakes on others
- The lifelong innate desire for belonging and engagement between a parent and child

We could say that all learning is about finding out what the consequences are for our actions. Developing personal responsibility requires learning this, including learning when the consequences are predictable or unpredictable. Our children will, by design, test their environments, test us, their parents, as well as their peers, teachers, and other adults. We all did this, and still do it. It is how we get to know each other.

Praise *n. An expression of approval, admiration, or favorable judgement.*

Praise is a little tricky. The value of praise depends on whether it is used as a form of reward – an extrinsic motivator (a strategy used to motivate) – or whether it is an authentic expression of appreciation, which satisfies belonging. Applauding your child's performance or accomplishment can build his self-confidence, enhance both self-appreciation and the acceptance of the appreciation given by others, as well as reinforcing his awareness of progress in growing abilities.

Frequently we parents use praise as a strategy (in order to make our children feel good or to motivate them to keep going). In doing so we may also give them inauthentic or inaccurate information. An example of inauthentic information is when we tell them what a good job they did, or that we are really happy they tried so hard, when we are actually disappointed or even upset. Make no mistake, they are aware when we are faking it. Experiencing this over time, children may adopt "fake liking," of things as well as people, as a legitimate adult survival skill. They may also be learning to distrust others' compliments. While there is nothing wrong with praise, I recommend replacing it with appreciation, a tool we'll discuss in the last chapter.

Choice and Choosing

One of our commonly adopted strategies for getting our young children to do what we want when we want them to do it, is to offer them two choices: a 'this or that' choice, perhaps coming from our susceptibility to the Law of Opposites (chapter 3, page 52). As a strategy for having our children learn to make and be responsible for their choices, it is not very useful (though it may be useful to us in the sense that at least we have some idea of some parenting thing to do in the moment). Did you ever notice that even when you have only one option, you can choose it or not? Consider that when you only have one option, and you have to do it, there is a certain quality to it (resistance?) and maybe even a certain kind of outcome that would be different if you actually chose to do it rather than complain and resist doing it. I am not saying it is better to accept everything. I am saying that choosing to accept an inevitable event or experience can change the quality of the experience, including allowing you to move on. I had to confront this for both myself and my six-year-old early one morning:

In the Face of No Choice

It was 5:30 AM and the telephone was ringing. I picked up the phone and heard the voice of the director of one our Maryland centers. She had a fever of 101 degrees and could not come in to open the childcare center, and her assistant director was out of town. I got up and started getting ready, thinking, "No problem ... Brynn can come with me to the center," as Carolyn was at work at the hospital and Brynn's school was closed for teacher conferences. Although I did not like having to get up so early unexpectedly, that was part of my job, and I did enjoy greeting staff, parents, and children in the mornings.

Brynn, who was eight at the time, woke up and got up, and I let her know we were going to go to the child care center.

Brynn: "I don't want to. I want to stay home."

Me: "Well, I'd like to stay home, too, sweetie, but we are going to go ... the director is sick and I am going to be her substitute today."

Brynn: "But I don't have to go ... I can stay home by myself!"

Me: "I know you can manage to stay home by yourself ... I trust you to take care of yourself and be safe most of the time. What doesn't work is that, if something unexpected happens, like a fire starts from a bad wiring, or if somebody comes to the door, and people find out that I left you home alone, do you know that the police could arrest me? That is because even though many children can take good care of themselves, some do not, and so there are laws and practices in communities that say what parents can and cannot do in order to protect families and children."

She listened to me, and we talked about why she didn't want to go, and I listened to her. I had no one to call at 6AM to ask for a non-emer-

gency favor, and I wasn't willing to take a risk leaving her home, and I said so.

Brynn cried and yelled and refused to go. I was momentarily stopped. I had never before had to force her to do anything, and I was dreading doing so. But I also knew something about choice, and about things we do have choices over and things we don't.

Me: "Brynn, you don't have a choice about going or not this morning... you and I are going. If I have to drag you to the car, I will do that. But you do have a choice about how you go, and how your day turns out when you go, and both are up to you. You can go, kicking and scream-ing, and not like going and have a terrible time. That's okay. You can also get yourself into the car and we can talk about what kinds of things you might like to do when we get there. I know all the teachers, and they are great, or, you can probably help out in office or in the two-year-old room – Miss Jan always likes to have you visit in her classroom. Those are all the choices I can think of at the moment. You can pick one or the other, and even change your mind."

There was only a slight change in her behavior, as I carried her to the car and buckled her in. She was thinking about it. By the time we got to the center, she was talking with me and remembered an incident when she visited the center when she was only three. At that time she was in a classroom with a new staff person who was struggling and ended up yelling at one of the kids before requesting assistance, and it scared Brynn. We talked about teachers and parents yelling, and about why that sometimes happens, and for some teachers, and some parents, and some children, it happens a lot. Brynn ended up helping Miss Jan in the class for two-year-olds, and, on the way home ...

Brynn: "I had the best day I ever had! Daddy, thank you for taking me."

Now you know everything I know about behavioral disciplinary strategies. And everything you and I know could become outdated at any time. But now you also know what to keep your eye on: your List A, your contexts, and workability (meaning, are you moving in the direction of your List A?) We have covered a lot of territory, and I expect that at least some, if not most, of it was new to you.

In the next chapter we are going to take a brief look at discipline, rules, and behavior. After that, in the last chapter, we'll finish with some new tools: tools that are designed to use in the new paradigm, and that will replace our old strategies.

XI. From Strategies to Tools

I'm not dumb. I just have a command of thoroughly useless information.

— Bill Watterson, cartoonist

Discipline and Misbehavior

Before we get in to using new tools, and why tools work and strategies don't, I want to just examine behavior with a wide lens. Is it okay with you for your child to get upset and kick you? Of course not. But let's break this down.

Like you, your child doesn't choose to get upset. Nothing is bad or wrong about getting upset – it is part and parcel of being a healthy functioning human being. However, if your child kicks you when he gets upset, that behavior is not likely on your List A (hurting or attempting to hurt others). His kicking may initially be out of his control, whether it is a new behavior or has become a strategy for gaining something. Whichever it is, he can learn to get that part of his behavior under control – especially if he is not concerned about losing your love and support. The presence of your unconditional love can make some of his strategic unworkable behavior unnecessary. You tell him that in your family it doesn't work for anyone to throw things, threaten others, or hurt others when they are upset, and that it is your job, as the parent, to be sure everyone is safe. Then you act in accordance with that – and as if nothing is wrong.

What you do about harmful, dangerous, or abusive behavior is this: you stop it as fast as you can, with a warning if there is time. Here is a sample warning: "You stop that now or I am going to stop you." You say it loud enough to be sure it gets her attention, and it is clear that you mean it. Then, after you have interrupted the behavior, you say, "It doesn't work in our family (or around me) for anyone to hurt or disregard anyone. You can count on me to be sure you and everyone else is safe, and I will do whatever I need to do to be sure of that." Again, no sternness, no niceness, no "do it or else!", just the facts. This creates a very safe place for your child to learn about behavior, including how to deal with being bullied or going along with it.

Characterizing harming people as bad or wrong behavior does not stop the behavior (otherwise people wouldn't be harming others, would they?). Stopping the behavior is what stops the behavior, and victimizers know that – and so should your children. Having a child feel guilty for being victimized may be entirely a result of the Good-Bad/Right-Wrong paradigm. It affects everyone within it. Example: You likely have heard, "Bad things don't happen to good people," or "I must have done something to deserve that."

Do we need to discipline our children when they persist in behaving in a way that doesn't work? And what do we mean by discipline, anyway?

There are two most frequently used meanings of discipline. Typically we mean the following:

> **Discipline** *n. the training of people to obey authorities, rules or a code of behavior, using punishment to correct disobedience*

v. To train someone to obey rules or agreed upon behavior, using punishment to enforce obedience; to punish or rebuke another officially for an offense

Clearly that definition puts the use of the word discipline into the old Good-Bad/Right-Wrong paradigm. But if we do not have discipline to get the behavior we want, what do we have? Rather than using rules, which require some form of discipline, or strategies, which are a form of force, we could use tools.

Rules as Tools

After I had started working in a preschool classroom I read about how some teachers in some schools encouraged the children to help make up the rules. In the 1970's and 80's it was common to encourage the children to participate in making up the rules, at least in the alternative schools I knew about. I tried this with a group of four-year-olds during the first week of one school year at one of our morning get-togethers.

I asked, "Okay, as you know, we have rules in school, and usually the teachers make them up. But I'm going let you help make them up. So... what do you think the rules should be?" And so they began:

"Don't hit",

"Don't yell",

"Don't take someone's crayons",

"Don't break someone's toy",

"You have to share the Legos",

"You have to share your cookies",

"No you don't",

"Yes you DO!"

I quickly realized they were already very familiar with the typical rules, and creating them all over again with them would only be a waste of time. I had thought this might help them "own" the rules as their own, but how unimaginative and unworkable this was going to be! We would have ten pages of rules — to be broken.

That night I thought a lot about what outcomes there might be, and for a while thought maybe I should set an arbitrary limit — like ten. I mean if God gave Moses ten commandments for humanity, we should be able to make preschool work with ten. If we let our young children make up the rules (having already adopted aspects of our adult thinking and applying it to the fullest), we'd be dealing with something like the IRS Code!

Then I imagined everyone either following or not following the rules and I realized that I pretty much knew beforehand who would and who wouldn't. So now what? I began to see some common aspects to all of the rules they listed, and I began to create my first List A, my list of what is really important to me as a parent and a teacher. What did I want the children to learn? What would they want to learn? I also noticed that I was assuming that we needed rules. Why? Well, that's a good question. Maybe I would find out something about their views and interests if I asked them the following questions:

What kind of school do you want to be in?

What do you like about being around other people?

What don't you like?

What do you want to learn about?

166

How do you want other people to treat you?

The more I thought about this, the shorter my list of rules became, and the more learning opportunities appeared. By the time I was ready to talk with the class, I had had another realization. The word "rule" itself already had some baggage. Today I would say we all have a context for rules — an attitude or a way we relate to them — and for many of us our attitude is similar. For example, we may think that rules are made to be broken, or that we get in trouble or are bad when we break them. Or we think that rules (at least the ones in front of us) are stupid. Or we just follow the rules no matter what, even when it doesn't seem fair or right. (More accurately, we follow the rules even when we notice it doesn't work in some way.) Just the phrase "break the rules" has a sense of wrongness to it. So what are rules, really? Why did I want to have rules? Later I realized that I too had been assuming, erroneously, that without rules children wouldn't learn to be civil and responsible.

I considered not having any rules. No one in my small preschool said we had to have them. I had read about schools that didn't have them. I imagined not having any. Given the relationship I had developed with my children, it didn't seem like rules would add any benefit. I brought this "no rules" idea up to my preschoolers. "Yea, no rules!" They were excited, and I was sure I had made a mistake! So then I said, "Well, if we do this then anyone can do whatever they want. For example, Danny [the biggest and hungriest kid in the class] could go ahead and eat anybody's lunch he wants to whenever he wants to. And, you know how much I like cookies!" I came up with a few more examples, and enthusiasm for 'no rules' dimmed. This lead me to the question, what are rules for? What do they actually do?

We typically use rules to try to make (or at best, encourage) the children to behave, be safe, or to keep order — but I saw something more useful. I began to think of them as tools. They are tools to help us work together, to feel safe and secure, to encourage us, to appreciate each other and our work. As with tools like a hammer and a saw, we could actually build a wonderful environment by using them. I really liked that the word 'tools' rhymes with 'rules' and the long "u" sound is spelled differently (I had discovered very early that inconsistency is always a great learning opportunity!). So I came back the third day – prepared.

First I asked my questions – what did they want? What was important to them about how they would like others to treat them and their work? I made sure they knew that having fun was okay and was a legitimate (today I would say "workable") desire in school.

I discovered that they already knew what they wanted and didn't want, once I showed them it was okay to want and not want things to happen around them, and to say something about it. Then I put up the list of twenty or so rules they had brainstormed earlier that week. I pointed out "don't hit" and "don't yell at people" and said, "These have something in common. I mean, if you don't hit someone and don't yell at them, you could say you are treating them with respect, right?" They agreed. It did sound good but I asked them, "What does respect mean to you?" Many had something to say along the lines of "you don't yell at someone", "you don't hurt them", "you act nice", etc. So I saw they already had some ideas about it – enough to proceed. I wrote down "treat each other with respect."

Then one asked, "What about 'don't tease anyone'? I don't like to be teased."

"Yes, that too. Let's write that one down. Now we'll cross out all the rules that we don't need anymore because they are part of treating others with respect, okay?" We did that, crossing off most of them.

Then we had "don't tear up someone's picture", "don't take someone's crayons", "don't wreck someone's Lego castle."

So I asked, "How about we add to this rule (about respect) and say 'Treat each other and each other's work with respect'?" They agreed again. More rules were crossed off.

A hand went up. "What about no spitting?" Aaron asked.

"Well, good question," I responded. "Spitting can spread germs — and who likes people to spit at them anyway — anybody here?" No hands went up. "So if I was spitting at you, would that be treating you with respect?"

"No."

So then I wrote "no spitting", and then crossed it off as it too came under the respect tool.

We still had a list of rules about no wasting paper, cleaning up, not breaking this or that toy or classroom material, washing our hands before snack and lunch. I asked, "If we had a tool that said 'take care of each other and our classroom', would that cover all these rules that are left? Let's see." And we went down the list and crossed off all the ones we didn't need any more. That left us with just a few from the original list.

One was, "Ask the teacher if you need to go to the bathroom," another was "Tell the teacher if someone is bothering you," and there were a couple of other similar ones. So I thought about this and came up with two tools for communication. One was, "If you want something, or you want something to happen, ask." I purposefully did not put in ask "the teacher." Many times I had observed the children helping each other, and that is much more empowering than getting the teacher to help when not needed. In our discussion we saw that making something stop happening was the same as making something else happen (replacement), so we could use one rule for both.

The other tool was, "If someone asks you something, answer." I came up with his last one as I noticed that certain children (and adults I knew, including myself!) could really control or avoid an uncomfortable situation if they didn't respond to someone asking for something. So I started with, "If you ask someone something, and they don't answer even though they heard you – is that 'treating you with respect'?"

They said "No."

In this process I discovered these kids had quite a complete operational understanding of the word "respect." They seemed to be aware of a kind of feeling associated with being treated with respect, and/or the feeling when they weren't. I also noticed there were times for almost all of them when they were not treating each other, or each other's work, with respect. For example, once in while one child would tease another. Sometimes that was okay – they would be having fun going back and forth, but sometimes the one being teased would get upset. Now they had a tool to stop the teasing: ask the teaser to stop teasing, and the teaser has a tool to create workability – answer. (Answering did not mean the teaser had to agree to stop; he could say, "I not going to stop", but that rarely happened).

Here are the tools we came up with:

* *Treat each other and each other's work with respect. (Their "work" was anything they created.)*
* *Take care of the classroom and everything in it.*
* *If you want something, or want something to happen, ask.*
* *If someone asks you a question, answer.*

These four tools covered everything. When there was a complaint about something, either I or one of the other kids would ask the person, "Did you ask?", or "Was laughing at her picture treating her with respect?", or, "Did you answer his question?" They would answer honestly. Just by asking, "Did you use our tools?", or, "Did she use our tools?" the children began to handle many more situations themselves.

They also noticed that when they used the tools, things worked the way they wanted. When they didn't use the tools, things didn't go the way they wanted. We all noticed that if something wasn't working, and if one person wasn't using one of the tools, it made perfect sense that there would be a problem. It was even an acceptable choice not to use the tools (as long as no one was hurt), and the solution was readily at hand. There was rarely a need for me to intervene, and I could focus on how to keep extending and expanding opportunities for learning and artistic expression.

Through this experience I learned that a goal for enhancing children's learning is to make a "teacher" less needed. My job was just to ask, "Did you use the tool for that?" or "What tool did you use?" or "Gee, too bad we don't have any tools for making that happen!" (Rolling my eyes along with giving a smile).

It was from watching these preschool children use these particular tools that I saw how much they wanted their lives to work, and how willing they were to be honest with each other – much more than I had been with my peers after a certain age, and much more than most adults I hung out with at the time.

How did I deal with a child who refused to use the tools? It depended. There is no right or wrong way, no one way. But most importantly I discovered that when a child was not willing to use a tool – that is, she continued to perpetuate an issue or problem – the reason was usually that she just couldn't see how she could 'win' (get what she ultimately wanted). Once she was invited to imagine what it would be like if others didn't use the tool either, she could see that it was really the only way and usually the fastest way to get what was important to her. Children are natural experimenters, so some of them are bound to think: "I wonder how long I can not use any of these tools?" And of course the answer would be, "As long as you can tolerate not getting what you really want." No resistance, and the consequences would just be the consequences.

At home, for families, these four classroom tools work well, too. How we help our young children learn to use them is just like help-ing someone use any tool, such as a hammer or saw. They require practice in real life, with real problems. Letting someone practice using a plastic hammer on a cardboard nail is interesting – for a short time. Developmentally appropriate environments may be necessary and useful at times, but even Mother Nature stretches our learning opportunities, imagination, perception, and all of our senses beyond our current abilities. That's part of an creating an enhanced learning environment.

Did I teach my two-year-old daughter to ask? I wouldn't use the word "teach." I asked whenever I wanted something, and I asked her to ask whenever she wanted something. Initially, her way of ask-ing was pointing and saying "ah ah ah." I got her what she wanted (if appropriate!). When she was a little older she'd say, "more milk." As I was getting the milk, I said, "The way to ask is like this: 'May I have some more milk?'" She immediately attempted to say that: "M-m-may ha- haf more milk?" Of course she could have more milk, either way. Withholding what children want, as a strategy, doesn't work any better than withholding love. If your child wants some-thing that you would want him to have, give it to him. Just say, mat-ter-of-factly, as you do that, "It works in our family to ask for what you want." After you have done this a few times, then wait and see if your child asks the next time. If not, ask him to ask. It is that simple and effortless.

Both Brynn and Auguste did try whining (someone told me many years ago that whining is a result of unexpressed anger, but who really knows?). I imitated the whining to Brynn, not to upset or make fun of her, but just so she could experience it herself. "Would you want Carolyn and me to whine to you for what we want?" She shook her head "no." "Just so you know, in our family, whining doesn't work." The next time she tried whining, I said, as I was heading for the refrigerator, "It works to ask, thank you." She stopped whining and asked. Children will adopt workable behavior in the absence of fear, control, embarrassment, and guilt; that is, in the presence of love and respect. There were many times, of course, when asking met with a "no" response. But we also talked about why we declined and often worked something out together.

Ending Misbehavior

Now is the time to get out your List B, your list of problematic behaviors and/or concerns. Pick one of them – probably one of your top three would work best. As you read this last chapter, have that problem or concern be what you use as the backdrop.

Notice, with regard to your specific issues, whenever you are thinking and/or feeling one of the following:

- I'm no good at this
- Someone or something is to blame
- Something is wrong
- The problem is beyond my ability and control
- Whenever you withdraw from a behavioral issue

One or more of these will occur every time you use a strategy or are assessing yourself within the Good-Bad/Right-Wrong paradigm. You will have just been or may still be upset about something. Your re-thinking and second-guessing tends to keep triggering your upset to some degree.

Here is a suggested initial process to follow to get back your fulfillment and satisfaction as a parent. This process follows draws upon
everything we have covered in the book:

1. Some behavior, perceived as a misbehavior, occurs.
2. Upset occurs: Notice its presence and impact, and that you
   didn't choose for it to happen.
3. Stop or don't start talking or acting out. Breathe until you
   have calmed down.
4. Observe: What happened? What expectation didn't happen?
   What paradigm is determining what you think and how you
   feel? (i.e., is something wrong somewhere?)
5. Expect your child to feel bad when she does a behavior that
   doesn't work when you are around. If your child is two or
   older, it is likely she has already learned from you that behaviors that you don't want her to do mean that she is bad, at
   least in your eyes. (Remember: though we may consciously
   disagree with this and even say so, the way the majority of us
   interact with our children gives the message that people *are*
   their behavior.)
6. Reassure your child that nothing is wrong, and that nothing
   that happened was bad. Say you are, or were, upset – if you
   are or were. Check it out with your child by asking: Did you
   think I was mad at you? Do you think you did something
   bad? Be honest. You can say, "You are right. I was mad, and I
   did act like you did something bad. But really, you didn't do
   anything bad. I just got upset when you broke the plate."
7. Restore (demonstrate) your love and acceptance for your
   child. It is about getting on eye level, attending to your tone,
   facial expression, openness of body language, and conversation, until you and your child feel close and reconnected.
8. Talk about what specifically happened, what didn't work,
   what you wanted instead, what could work next time, and
   again say that nothing that happened was bad or wrong. If
   there is a previously agreed upon consequence for what

happened, remind your child, and then deliver it. Tell him that you are delivering it because you said you would and not because he did anything bad. Accept any appropriate apologies, and coach him on inappropriate apologies (Example: "I'm sorry I cried, Mommy." Say: "You don't have to apologize for your feelings, Jimmy. It is okay to cry or get mad. What didn't work is that you were standing on the chair and reaching for the cookie jar instead of asking." Neither of you need apologize for getting upset. Tell him, however, "Being mad is not an excuse for hurting, scaring, or making fun of someone. It is okay to be mad when you are mad. But hurting, scaring, or making fun of someone doesn't work.")

9. Ask for a promise with regard to what happens next time.
10. Show your appreciation for your child's willingness to engage, forgive, and work together with you.

At first glance, this looks like a long process. The first time or two it may take three to four minutes. After you have done it a just a few times it will move much faster. Once you and your child are familiar with it, the whole process can take 30 seconds – no kidding. Here is an estimated breakdown: With a little practice, numbers 1 – 3 will take 5 – 10 seconds. Number 4 will take about 20 seconds. Numbers 6 and 7 will take as long as they take, but note that the more you do this, the faster the restoration will take, and at some point, it will begin to happen automatically and even instantly. Numbers 8 and 9 may take a minute or two. Number 10 will initially involve saying those things out loud, but soon merely a wink will say it all.

When you do this, stay on purpose. Making this a longer-than-necessary or social conversation could encourage unworkable behavior. As soon as the conversation is over, move on to what you were doing just before the incident started. If your child resists promising to choose a workable plan, then set up a consequence for the next occurrence (follow the guide described under Consequences in the next chapter, "A Box of New Tools"). In between occurrences of persisting unworkable behaviors, look for opportunities to demonstrate and talk about alternatives that work that you have seen or done (not as a lecture, but as a sharing of your experience).

Just like riding a bike, this process will begin to occur automatically after you make it a regular practice. Of course, that requires having your child do and say things that don't work (otherwise, no practice!), which is another way of saying that it requires that your child be fully engaged in her own learning and development. But that is an innate drive, so it will happen anyway. And as your child learns about behavior and develops a deep intrinsic value for work-ability, she will have fewer unworkable behaviors at home and will likely want to take on larger social issues in her life outside her family later on.

What follows next are some tools for you to use and master, and hopefully you will keep inventing new ones with your children. Context matters, and 'adventure' is a context. Consider that trying them out is an adventure, to share with your child.

XII. A Box of New Tools

*F*or *the things we have to learn before we can do them, we learn by doing them.*

– Aristotle

Context

Context, with regard to behavior, is everything. The freedom to learn, both as a child in the world, and as a parent, is context-dependent. The most empowering context you can create as a parent is a context of unconditional love and support for your child, and to re-create it every time time the Good-Bad/Right-Wrong paradigm grabs you. And it will – frequently. It will cause love, joy, and intimacy to retreat – until you recreate the context of unconditional love and support. We could say that what works is to welcome the Good-Bad/Right-Wrong paradigm as a reminder, and then create a context of unconditional love and support (using all your languages).

The reason for sharing any intentional context with your children is to help them understand and be able to relate to you and behavior, and begin to see that who people are at heart is not their behavior.

Here are two examples of possible ways for a parent to verbalize contexts with their child.

Context for Cooperative Behavior-Responsibility: "Your behavior is up to you, and every behavior either works for you and other people or it doesn't. What we do in our family is find a way for things to work for everyone, even if someone doesn't like it. It is my job to be sure that how we act and what we say works for all of us. You can count on me to let you know what is working and what is not, but the choice is up to you. And you can let me know what is working for you and what is not, too. I love you no matter what you choose."

Context for Workability-Schooling: "People are brilliant and able, and that means you are, too. There is nothing being taught in your school that you cannot learn easily. If something is hard for you, it works to ask for help and support. I will always find a time to listen and support all the learning you can get both in school and out of school as well. Learning happens everywhere. And if you are bored or get too distracted, it works to tell me that, too. Right now, it works for our family for you to be in school and doing well. If you have or ever have a reason for not doing well, that is okay, and let's talk about it."

You can create a context for any circumstance, at any time. Within the new What Works/What Doesn't Work paradigm, and in a context of unconditional love, support, and respect, any problem between you and anyone else, especially your children, can be resolved. What follows are some conversational and behavioral tools that I found useful.

Appreciation

Appreciation *n. The recognition and sharing of the qualities of someone or something valued* *v. (Appreciate) To show gratitude to someone or for something.*

Appreciation as a tool, rather than a strategy, is not an assessment of whether your child was good or bad, or a pointing out of something missing. It is not used "in order to get" your child to do anything. It is an the expression of your gratitude. Here are some not-so-common but possible examples of verbal appreciation for something specific:

- "I appreciate the way you thanked Daddy for helping you clean your room. You are awesome."
- "Mary's mom told me she likes it when you visit Mary because you play so well together."
- "I'm sorry you didn't make the team, Alice ... and I'm proud of you for your courage."

You can also appreciate the potential within your child. A good friend and author, Rick Ackerly[54], calls this potential your child's "genius," from the original Latin derivation meaning "attendant spirit present from birth, innate ability or inclination." This kind of appreciation occurs when you are "watering a seed" that is already planted, or inviting your child's inner desire to learn, to discover, to contribute, to come out and play. Here are some examples:

- "I love you for no reason ... you are such a lovable person. I'm glad I'm your Dad."
- "Thank you for being just the way you are!"
- "I love the way your drawing shows me new ways to see things."
- "I feel really good about how it is okay with you for us to talk about anything. That's the best gift I can imagine."

---

54 *Ackerly, Rick, The Genius in Every Child, Lyons Press, Guildford, CT, 2012*

If you attempt to use appreciation to compensate for a lack of something or to get your child to do something (as a strategy), it is inauthentic and your child will likely perceive it as such. If some expected or desired behavior is missing and it is on your mind, say so. Say it as just a thought you have, as a concern that you want to check out. Saying what is on your mind as a concern gives your child information about you, a "place" to stand, from which it is not only safe but potentially valuable to seek feedback and explore ideas.

One of the most common complaints I've heard from parents is that their children show no appreciation for all that they do for them. Your showing your appreciation creates a context in which they can show their appreciation of you. And in this context, when you want appreciation, it works to ask for it.

Consequences

As we saw in the previous chapter, the Good-Bad/Right-Wrong paradigm turns our parent-generated consequences into punishments, and as such they were at best a temporary and frequently not a very fulfilling solution. Withholding dessert, play time, videos, even the revered "time out" and it's more PC cousin, the "time in," are typically not fulfilling nor relationship-building. But this is only due to the nature of the Good-Bad/Right-Wrong paradigm on their set up and delivery, not because consequences aren't useful learning opportunities.

Now that we know a little about how our children learn, and what drives their behavior to a large degree, we can ask this question: When should I set up a consequence, and when not?

Two Kinds of Behavior

Consider that your child has two kinds of behavior – experimental (to learn from) and strategic (already learned; to use for something). Why is it important to distinguish one from the other? Because the way we deal with a behavior that doesn't work depends on which of these it is.

1. Experimental (explorative, scientific) – This is a new behavior or experiment. It may or may not get a desired result, from your child's point of view. As an experiment, he will find out what happens when he does X, and, as with every behavioral choice we make, something always happens; there are always consequences. The consequences may be extremely desirable, extremely undesirable, or somewhere in between. Your young child does not think of this behavior as an experiment – he just does it because it is a way to find out about the world. The younger the child, the more often her behavior is experimental, the more often her choices of behavior don't work for us. A child may not know how important it is that Mommy gets to work on time, and telling him that "it is important" or "because I have to" doesn't mean much to him. Mommy, at some point, may want to fill in the details of why she goes to work, and why it works to get there on time, so he can begin to understand her view.

2. Strategic – This a behavior that has passed the experimental stage and now is an applied strategy: your child gets, at some level or for some drive, a desired result. A behavior may become strategic even if it only sometimes gets the desired result, as sometimes may be more desirable than than no times. When a child discovers that doing X "works" (at least sometimes) to get Y – a desirable result in his view – then X becomes a "strategic" behavior. Your little scientist tested it. We might try on a view that any persistent behavior has been

learned (i.e., inadvertently taught by us). If we can see how they learned it from us, then we can undo it, sometimes without setting up a consequence but just by expanding the child's view (of what is happening). We do that by sharing our view, as well as whatever consequences occurred that we know of but that he does not. It's easy to address and undo it: We tell them how we taught them that behavior, and that we found out that what we taught them doesn't work. We reveal our own learning process, mistakes and failures as well as successes. We role-model that it is okay to be vulnerable (to appear imperfect). It is next to impossible for us to undo any of our child's unworkable behavior if we act like we had nothing to do with how it was learned in the first place. But if we adopt the view that it was learned, we are moving past memories from being implicit to being explicit; that is, from being "the truth" to be something we learned[55]. And then we can choose to not repeat what doesn't work.

We can use a consequence to have our child choose a workable behavior over a strategic behavior that doesn't work for us.

Now a second question: How do we make a consequence a learning opportunity and keep it from becoming a punishment?

We start by seeing how physical-world consequences work, such as gravity. One key difference between you and I, and gravity, is that you and I care about the choices our children make, and gravity doesn't. I don't propose that we attempt to change that difference. But we can, in the What Works/What Doesn't Work paradigm, set up a consequence and deliver it in such a way that our child has no fear of loss of our love and support no matter which choice he makes: he is free to choose.

---

55 Review "Implicit Memory" on page 63.

What works when dealing with experimental behavior is to have a conversation about the workability of it from everyone's point of view. Ask your child, did it work? Did you get what you want? If he says no, that will likely be the end of it. If he says yes, ask him, "what was it you wanted?" Let him answer. Then let him know what didn't work for you. Ask him if he would find something that works for both of you, or let him know he can ask you for ideas. If nothing works for that behavior, then say that.

Note: Role-model respect – listening, responding authentically and with trust – in your conversations. Always end your behavioral conversations with, "Remember, your behavior is up to you. I love and will support you no matter what. If you don't stop doing something harmful, you can count on me to stop you. But whatever you do, I love you and will support you the best way I know how. You are great, and *great people sometimes do things that don't work.*"[56]

Consider that a behavior that becomes strategic does so because it works in some way from the view of a child's brain. Remember, young children are both brilliant and ignorant. Some misinterpretation, or some perceived lack of fulfillment of some drive or desire, is what causes a behavior to persist. That is, there may be some perceived value or need being fulfilled by the way in which you have been responding to it that you (or anyone else) cannot see or understand. You don't need to know what it is, however. Just change the way you have been responding. Change your tone, your decibels, in the opposite direction of where they have been. Get louder or softer, get more or less serious. Experiment. Sometimes this works, and more often than we might expect. However, if it doesn't work, then do the following.

---

56 This last statement I first heard from Philp N. Adams, president and founder of Child's Play Learning Centers, Inc. It is a powerful statement from a parent to a child.

Find or request a private time with your child after she has done the specific unworkable behavior you want to address. Attend to your context: Use a non-confrontive tone, get down on eye level, be warm, open and honest. Leave any strategy of being nice, stern, or overly talkative behind. Then, with your child present, recall the conversation you had together the first time the unworkable behavior occurred, and whether your child said he would do what works or not. Point out again, briefly, what it is about the behavior that doesn't work. Then ask again whether she would be willing to do what works the next time. Younger children will tend to agree and then not do it, usually because they forget or because they are focused on what they are doing, and less so on the workability of it for others. Older children, sometimes due to their resignation in the face of dealing with ongoing parental upsets, may resist and say they won't do what works. In either case, listen and say that you heard what she said, and if she agrees to do what works, thank her. If you get resistance, just tell her that it is up to her and that you aren't going to force her, and, there will be a consequence. In either case, say that, no matter what happened in the past, "the consequence will happen if you do what doesn't work the next time." Then tell her that the consequence will happen only because you said it would happen, and not because the behavior is bad or wrong. Tell her that whether the consequence happens or not is up to her — it is her choice to do what works or what doesn't. Then end with, "Whatever you do, I love you and will support you the best way I know how. You are great, and great people sometimes do things that don't work." Keep being aware of your tone, your facial expression, and body language. (Smiling might be kind of weird, but being stern-faced is part of the non-verbal language of the old paradigm.) A three or four-year-old child would likely be in your lap.

The Delivery of a Consequence

The delivery is also about the context: nothing is wrong, and neither your child nor her behavior was bad. She did what didn't work, and she knew ahead of time what would happen. Since she did what didn't work, and doesn't want the consequence, she is testing you. Decide to pass with flying colors. Be light, be honest, be accepting, and follow through with the consequence every time. She may try every one of her own strategies to get you to get mad or give up. Just observe her. Be interested in how she learned and why she tries the strategies. See if any are ones you have used on her. Know that by not giving in you are showing her that her strategies are bankrupt, and only through open conversation with you will she get what she really wants – your loving engagement and appreciation of what she has been through. And deliver the consequence. Later you can tell her that you appreciate all that she's been through. You don't have to act as though you like delivering or dislike delivering the consequence. Just deliver it. And remember, the purpose of the consequence is not to make her change her behavior – it is to build her trust of herself and her trust of you. "Why do I have to have this consequence?!" "Because that's what I said would happen if you chose that behavior again."

When the consequence is over, don't make a big (or even a small) deal about it. Let it be over. Move on. You are always available to role-model behavior that works, and holding on to past behaviors really doesn't help anyone move forward.

Integrity

There is another tool that is required for consequences to be consequences, and that tool is *integrity* – doing what we said we would do. A usable (that is, predictable) physical world consequence such as gravity, you can count on it, every time. That allows us to make choices with regard to it, and use it in ways to further our endeavors. This is the goal we can have for our parent-generated consequences in the What Works/What Doesn't Work context. When we do not follow through on a given consequence, our child will henceforth not know in the future whether a consequence we set up will happen, causing uncertainty. This changes the nature of a consequence into a threat. Uncertainty is the enemy of a sense of safety – our hindbrain becomes more active, more in control, as it monitors for danger.

Also, when we define integrity as a tool rather than a moral judgment, we parents have the freedom to fail, which means we also have the freedom to learn and develop our own personal responsibility, free from the fear of being bad or wrong ourselves.

Whether we are talking about building an office building or building a business or building a relationship, integrity is an essential ingredient. Integrity allows things to work, but doesn't by itself cause them to work. Other specific actions may be required, and sometimes not.

Here is a good example of the beauty and power of integrity:

The Field Trip

At a staff meeting one day during my first year of working at the Amazing Life Games community preschool, we decided to take the kids on a field trip. We would go to a great outdoor playground at Haine's Point in Washington, D.C. – where the Anacostia River meets the Potomac River, near the National Mall. We would go the following week. And I would drive the van.

Over the next few days it seemed that I was much more excited about going than the other staff. Having never been on a preschool field trip before, I listened to the other teachers and watched their responses to it. The more I thought about it, the more I realized there was a lot a pressure to be sure the children were safe (of course), that they behaved appropriately, and that no child got lost or left behind. The consequences for missing something (or worse, someone), could be severe. So the next morning, being the driver, I got to "work" on it. I had a meeting with the class of three and four-year-olds about the rules. They already had a good idea from either earlier field trips or riding in the car with their parents: no yelling, no hitting, no sticking their arms out the window — pretty basic stuff. I could see that knowing "the rules" would not solve the problem that we, the staff, would have to deal with. They knew the right answers, but still field trips were typically difficult. It wasn't a knowledge issue, it was a behavior issue. Somehow even back then I sensed that the way to find out how to handle it successfully, and have fun, would be to ask the children. So I asked "Why not yell?" "Because its too loud!" someone offered. "Just because!" someone else said. "Because it hurts my ears!" was another response.

I said, "Well, okay, all that may be true. But here are some more reasons. I'm driving and it is important that I keep us safe, and to do that I need to see out the front and back windows, and hear what's going on outside. It's my job to be sure we are all safe. If someone got hurt on the field trip because we acted in an unsafe way, do you think we would go on any more field trips?"

"N-o-o," they said.

"Do you think your parents would let you go on any more field trips?"

"N-o-o," they said.

"Right," I said. "And I don't want anyone to get hurt or have a bad time on the trip, either. And, do you ever want to go on any more field trips?"

"Yes, yes!", they said.

"Okay — me too! So it's up to all of us, right? I mean, do we teachers stand up and yell or hit each on the bus?"

"No...", they said almost in unison.

"Do you?" I asked. A moment of silence. Then a few "nos", then a "sometimes" and "I don't but he does", and even an "I do!" I thanked them for being honest with me, and made no comments on their answers.

Then I said this: "You know, I want to go to Haines Point... in fact I like to go a lot of places... but not if I'm not going to have fun. It isn't fun for me if I have to keep telling someone 'stop doing this' or 'stop doing that' – like going out of sight of us, or running ahead of the rest of us, or lagging behind when it is time to go. Do you have fun when we teachers are upset and yelling?"

"No," they said. And one piped up, "Yes..." I looked at her and smiled. "Yes, I think a lot more people than we think sometimes like making other people frustrated. Thank you for telling me that."

"Well... in either case, teachers don't like it. So I suppose you might get to go on a lot more trips with us and with your parents if we all have fun when we go. What do you think?"

"Uh-huh."

"So its up to you – it really is. We teachers can go to the museum any-time we want, but you can't, not yet. So how do we make this work so we can go on lots more field trips this year?"

We made a list of rules that would keep us safe on the trip. Then I said, "What happens if you "break" a rule?"

"You get in trouble."

"No-o", I said.

"You go in time-out."

"No-o", I said, "What happens is — we turn around and come back. It's about all of our safety." They were silent, like waiting for something else to be said. "I mean it," I said. Then I said, "Is it a deal? Do you agree?"

They said "Okay".

Then I said, "Is there anyone who doesn't agree to this?"

One boy asked, "But what if I forget?"

"Someone will remind you. And if then you don't stop doing whatever you are doing that doesn't work, we turn around and come back — all of us. Okay?"

"Okay," they said. Again, one courageous soul piped up with, "What if I don't want to come back and I didn't do anything?"

"Good question," I responded. "I wouldn't want to come back either. But safety is most important, and we are all in this together. If we have to come back, how many of you would be disappointed?" All hands went up. "Whoa ... then we'll all be disappointed."

We loaded up the van and the extra cars and everyone was excited and talking. Just before we started to drive, I reviewed our agreement and what happens if we all do not keep the field trip rules. After a few blocks a reminder or two was necessary, and that was all that was needed. But after a couple of miles, just after we got onto Rock Creek Parkway, a couple of kids got into an argument, and started poking at each other and calling each other names. They got a reminder, which didn't make any difference. I pulled off Rock Creek Parkway and into a parking area. They knew something was up — you could hear a pin drop. One of the chaperones said she would move the kids who were "acting up" next to her. I said, "No, don't do that. Let them sit where they are. We are going back to school just like we agreed we would." I then stood up and faced the kids. I said, "I know most of you were doing what works, and thank you very much... that was great. And some of you weren't, and we agreed we'd go turn around and go back, and so that's what we're going to do – because we said we would. And by the way, no one is in trouble – we are just going back to school." And that's what we did.

It was a relatively silent ride back to school. Even the other teachers were silent. Later one said that she was surprised that I did that. I let her know that I was too, and that I really was disappointed that we didn't get to go, but was already wondering what would happen on future field trips.

We arrived back at school. Later, when parents' found out that we didn't go, they first asked asked us why. I smiled and said, ask the children. When a parent asked, they replied, "We didn't do what worked." There was no blame or animosity towards the ones who didn't keep our behavioral agreements, and that seemed to rub off on the parents. And that was the last field trip we ever came back early from because of behavior that didn't work in the van. No time-out needed, no lecture, nothing but doing what we said.

Could you "hear" what worked in that story? Can you see why it doesn't work when we add our reprimands, our "teaching" comments, our ways of "helping" (moving a child to sit with a teacher, in this example)? Can you now see why those things keep our children from learning? In retrospect, I see that we gave all the power of going or not going to the children, yet we staff remained in charge in a responsible way.

Requests

Making clear and respectful requests is an art. Some parents don't think children should be asked to behave, only *told* to behave. I have been asked many times, "Why ask your child to do X if they don't really have a choice?" And I have to remind myself there is no right or wrong way to do this. Making requests of others is a social skill, and so much more valuable than the traditional boss/employee roles. Asking is not about relinquishing power. Asking effectively and powerfully is about workability, both in the moment and later in life. For me, I want children around me to make choices, whether they work or do not work. And if their choice works, I can authentically say, "Thank you – I appreciate that." If it doesn't work, I then have a choice also. Is there a consequence of a child's choice that doesn't work for him, one that he is already experiencing? Why would my interrupting that be useful? And if his choice of behavior worked for him (apparently) and not for me or for others, then what response could I give that would offer the most valuable learning opportunity? Whether as a parent, teacher, or employer, I decide. In the What Works/What Doesn't Work, I can learn to be as personally responsible as I choose. And those around me will learn from me.

Notice if you have a pre-existing expectation that your child will say "yes" or "no" or will ignore you. Your expectation will color your request if you don't notice that it is there. When you ask, being nice or being stern sends a message that complicates your child's decision-making process. If you are really nice, their choosing "no" can load them up with guilt, and if they choose "yes," they may think that you think they are just being nice in return (and maybe they are). If you are stern in your request, it might sound like you don't trust them to cooperate (and while you may have good reasons from the past to not trust them with regard to cooperating, it is time to give that up if you want that to change). Just ask, for example, "Beth, would you ("please" is optional) not yell in the same room I am in?" No begging, no force, no bribery ("If you agree, I'll..."). But here are two things to do when asking: make warm and open eye-contact, and then wait for a clear answer, with eye-contact. Once you become adept in the new paradigm, this way of gaining cooperation will become the norm. They will ask as respectfully as you do.

If your child has shown persistent opposition to any specific requests you have made in the past, you may not want to take time in the moment to deal with a "no." I still recommend that you ask your child, however. But use the following form: "Beth, would you be willing to help me set the table in a few minutes?" This "would you be willing to" phrase lets you find out where Beth is about helping without making her choose to help or not. There is less of a perception of force (especially if you have used a forceful tone in the past). After she responds, then you can decide whether it works better for you to go forward without her help now and address her unwillingness later. Unwillingness, by the way, sometimes may occur as a way to "get even" for a past forced response, or for not having been appreciated for cooperation in the past, or because there is no perceived value for cooperating. Each of these reasons can be cleared up by you if you are willing to give up that your child shouldn't need to be appreciated for helping out, that he should just do it. No matter what you think about this idea, the "shoulds" reveal the mischievous impact of the old Good-Bad/Right-Wrong in the matter.

"Anne, Would You Be Willing to Set the Table?"

A mom in one of my first workshops tried using "Would you be willing to set the table?" with her seven-year-old daughter, Anne. She said Anne always had said "No" to her when she asked her to set the table, and then things went downhill from there. A year or so later I ran into her in a local store, and she said, "Marty, that 'would you be willing' phrase made the biggest difference in our relationship. I went home from that workshop and asked, 'Anne, would you be willing to set the table for dinner?' and she said, 'Okay.' And she's done it every time I've asked since then. Thank you so much for that."

The way we ask others makes a difference, even when we use words that sometimes "work" better, such as "would you be willing." We do have a kind of request that works quite well when our child's choice, yes or no, works either way for us. We call it an invitation. This is when we invite someone over for dinner, or to go to a movie with us. They can decline freely, with no cost to our relationship in the moment (though we may afterwards wonder why they have declined the last ten invitations with rather "weak" excuses, though even in that case it is not the invitation that caused the problem).

"No"

The word "no" is one of the most loaded words in a family in a child's early years. A child does not like to hear the word "no," and neither does a parent, but for entirely different reasons. For a child, initially a "no" only means she isn't going to get or do what is wanted in the moment, by either herself or her parent. But later there is possibly a both threatening and surprising reaction. For a parent, hearing "no" from his child, especially frequently, is usually taken as a form of opposition or disobedience, though her child initially may be just experimenting.

Consider that the first use of the word "no" by a two-year-old is actually a first step in learning personal responsibility. It is a developmental milestone in the sense that a parent will soon no longer be heard automatically as a Big People (who can do no wrong and who knows everything). Saying "no" is a unique experience of budding self-determination. Suddenly, or perhaps not so suddenly, a child "awakens" to his own power. He can say "no!" and that saying it really has an impact on his circumstances (and parents!). He will find opportunities to use it just to keep seeing what happens, and that can be a great learning opportunity.

What is "no"? When you say "no" aren't you simply saying that you don't want some thing or you don't want to do some activity? It is a communication of a "not" wanting. And if the other person says, "Aw, come on, you'll like it!" you can then refuse with another "no," which is another level of communication, or you can say, "Okay, I'll do it." While it may seem that there is obviously nothing wrong or bad about saying "no," I have found that both many children and adults have difficulty "just saying 'no'." Why is this? Consider that, when we were very young – three or four – our saying "no" to our parent was seen as a threat to their being in control. And their response was seen by us as a threat to our relationship with them, and that is what was wired into our implicit memory bank. We have a sense that we are getting disapproval and are bad, especially if we have no good reason or explanation for saying "no" readily available. Thus, "no" does not just mean "no."

After I had noticed this in my preschoolers, I planned a exercise that raised their awareness of their own and others' ways of saying "yes" and "no." We sat in a circle. I had a ball in my lap. We practiced asking for the ball and being asked for the ball. The person who was asked got to say "yes" a few times, and "no" a few times. There was a huge variation in tone, in facial expression, and body language, both when they were asked and when they said "yes" or "no." We talked about all of that, and soon they were able to just say "yes" or "no", as if "yes" just meant "yes" and "no" just meant "no." As a parent, be thinking about how you can show your child that, for you, "no" just means "no," and along with that, "no" *means* "no" (rather than "maybe" or "later" or "yes if you keep bugging me"). Any explanation doesn't change the meaning, but could be a learning opportunity.

Why is this important? It was on my List A that my girls could say "no" to anyone about anything without needing a good reason, and I want that for my grandchildren – in fact, for all children.

Acceptance

The most useful definition of love I ever heard was this: to love someone means to accept them just as they are and just as they are not. Think about this. One of our most common identity threats is "What will happen if I change (grow, learn, accept new ideas, etc.)? Will I still be loved? Will I still have friends?" The best gift you can give your child is permission and support for growth and change. You give this gift as a verbal commitment: "I love you no matter what, and I always will. Even if I get angry, afraid, sad, or concerned about you or something you tell me, I will love you. And even if at times I don't do what you might want me to do, I will love you. And if you ever question that, be sure and ask me, okay?"

XIII. Conclusion

Our Elders have created for us a sacred way of being in the universe. It is our responsibility to pass this understanding on to the next generation.

— *Tessie Naranjo (Pueblo of Santa Clara), 2001*

The quality and future of your parenting is now in your miraculous hands. You have new tools for being with your children, and in your family. Practicing using them works. Failure works just as much as success, as long as you are asking "what worked" and "what didn't work," and exploring together what you could do differently. For example, remember that hammer mentioned in the Preface? It doesn't matter whether you hit the nail or not, you learn with every swing. You can and do determine the local paradigm in which your family lives, learns, and converses. You can adopt or make up new contexts and paradigms. You can make up new meanings for old behaviors and reactions, and your new meanings will be adopted or improved upon in the conversations you have about them with your family members. You can use your "hammer" (these tools and the What Works/What Doesn't paradigm) to build the "house" (your family life, environment, and context) that you want to inhabit — and in which your children will thrive.

Parenting will still be challenging. If it weren't, it would not be so rewarding. By using these tools you can meet any challenge in satisfying and fulfilling ways.

Why else is this book important? It is bigger than the quality of life of just my family or your family. We live in an incredibly diverse and, in many ways, an unpredictable world. It includes both workability and unworkability. We live in a world that also includes separation into the good and the bad, the right and the wrong, the ones who belong and ones who do not. It is a world in which we have tried to resolve issues defined by hindbrain thinking, using force, threat, and fear. We have clung to strategies from the past, a kind of "stickiness" to the rightness of our past thinking and responding. We could just notice the messages from our hindbrain and, if we notice a moment of choice, pause – whether that be before, during, or after our reactions. Then we can keep our unfathomable cortex informed so it can do its work – to solve complex problems with other people, both locally and globally. And in moments of personal challenge, creativity, and even breakdowns, when we share ourselves and what is happening, our children then get to express their love and support for us, and we for them. Together we can grow and solve complex problems with a view towards what works and what doesn't work, in cooperation with one another over the course of our lives.

Where is the tipping point for human society?[57] How many parents would it take to have enough children grow up knowing that human beings, working together, can solve any problem? How many generations? How can we shorten the number? What can you do? What will you do? As a parent, you are already engaged in something that

---

57 "When just ten percent of the population holds an unshakable belief, their belief will always be adopted by the majority of the society," say scientists at Rensselaer Polytechnic Institute, in "Minority Rules: Scientists Discover Tipping Point for the Spread of Ideas," http://news.rpi.edu/update.do?artcenterkey=2902

affects future generations. What kind of impact do you want to have – every day?

I wish you and your family great success in making the kind of difference that you want to see in the world around you as you create an adventurous life full of joy, peace, and love!

Take good care of yourself. Take good care of your dreams.

Nothing has a stronger influence psychologically on their environment and especially on their children than the unlived life of the parent.

– C.G. Jung

Appendix I

Parent Lists (Most Common Items)

List A: What Results Do You Really Want for Your Children from Your Parenting?

- Have a passion for things in life and for life itself.
- Be comfortable in his/her own skin.
- Be empathetic, curious, observant, and creative.
- Have a sense of wonder and awe about the world.
- Appreciate the value of planning for the future.
- Successfully follow his/her dreams and heart.
- Have a strong social "compass."
- Treat others with dignity and respect.
- Appreciate people and other living things.
- Think for him/herself.
- Be able to act independently.
- Know that s/he is loved and is lovable.
- Love others unconditionally.
- Be forgiving of him/herself and others.
- Participate in his/her community.
- Have fun, laugh, and be playful.
- Maintain a joyous relationship with his/her family.

List B: What Should or Shouldn't Be Happening?

"I would always (or never) ..."

- Be able to give up control.
- Be an impeccable role model.
- Be able to make more time for myself.
- Know the answer to every "Why?" question.
- Be fully organized and use great time management skills.
- Have peace and endless reserves of patience.
- Never get upset.
- Not experience any stress.
- Be comfortable with conflict.
- Not be so tired.
- Be able to come up with great educational activities every day.
- Never yell at my children.
- Enjoy having extended family visit us.
- Have time to do things I like to do.
- Interact more with other families in my neighborhood.

"My child would always ..."

- Be cooperative.
- Do what I need them to do when I need them to do it.
- Not fight or argue or tease each other.
- Be willing to help me clean up around the house.
- Eat well-balanced meals.
- Want to have extended family around more.
- Always behave in public and never embarrass me.

List C: What Are Your Current Disciplinary Strategies?

What do you do now (what strategies do you use)?

- Beg
- Give them two choices
- Negotiate
- Time out or time in
- Get very serious or stern
- Bribe with goodies
- Guilt trip(bribe with emotions, act hurt or let down)
- Reward
- Count to 3
- Take away toys or activities
- Ignore
- Distract
- Threaten or scare
- Ask extra nicely
- Show disapproval
- Get help

Appendix II

Three Brains, Three Functions

Cortex (New actions, workability, risk-assessment)

- Follows instructions and answers questions
- Imagines possible futures (visualizes what was and is not yet)
- Solves problems
- Grows in size and strength with use
- Evaluates messages from lower brains based on the perceived reality and severity of a potential threat, and our desired future

Mid Brain (Emotions, motivations)

- Gets sensory messages from hind brain
- Interprets combinations of internal sensations (degrees of sensation, pain) as emotions, based on early learning (fear, upset, joy, etc.)

Hind Brain (Past circumstances, survival reactions)

- This-or-that, you-or-me, us-or-them viewpoint for action
- Compares current experience with past-based experience
- No thinking or visualizing
- Creates automatic survival response relative to perceived past threat

- Sends sensory messages to limbic brain
- Sends directives that bypass conscious decision-making by .5 to 1.5 milliseconds

Appendix III

Reflections on Terms

educate: The following was a response from a friend and linguist, Kevin Kautz, when I asked about the meaning of educate, as I had much preferred the meaning "to lead out" when I consider myself an educator.

There are many websites that claim that educate means "to lead out" in Latin. But this is not correct.

There are two Latin verbs, <<educare>> and <<educere>>. When you conjugate the verb, the common form <<educo>> is identical (Latin homonyms). What happens over time is that as such words are borrowed into other languages such as Old English, those distinctions can become blurred. And later, such as happens now, people who don't take the time to carefully research this will follow the wrong (!) path and miss the distinction.

So what we have is this – there is one etymology of "lead out" which is where we get the obscure English word "educe" which means "to bring out" ... typically used as "to bring out of someone a talent that they had but were not aware of." This is not the derivation of education, but you can see why it would appeal to many people to think that it is. This is where the "lead forth" or "lead out" derivation belongs. The

Latin <<educere>> means "to lead forth", "to lead out", or "to bring out". All of the meanings related to leading are coming from <<educere>>. This is also the source for the Italian "IL DUCE" (the leader), which was the common term for Mussolini.

The second etymology, which is the true derivation of "educate", is from the other source. The Latin <<educare>> means "to nurture", "to bring up", "to rear young", or occasionally, "to produce." There are no connections to leading when you start from <<educare>>.

So in spite of many websites that confuse or combine the two... the English word "educate" started in Latin as "to bring up" (as in nurturing or rearing young).[58]

therapy: I am not a therapist. My work is educational behavioral enlightenment ("bringing light to behavioral issues"). Rather than fixing something that is broken or wrong, leading something out, or bringing something forth, like an inherent quality within a person, I propose views that allow parents and teachers to see behavioral situations in ways that result in opportunities and the freedom to accomplish their intrinsic goals in their families and classrooms.

self-worth: "another term for self-esteem" [Merriam-Webster Online]

Yet esteem and worth have different definitions. Thus, I would redefine the word self-worth, and not use the word self-esteem, when talking about how a person values him- or herself, no matter how they are treated by others. An intrinsic self-worth is a more consistently useful concept, as self-esteem tends to be more as others perceive one. My view is that people who experience being worthy – having an internalized value or worthiness – tend to take good care of themselves. Their worthiness shows, no matter what others think.

---

58   Personal e-mail from Kevin Kautz, contributor and linguist

We can attempt to increase a person's self-esteem by using teaching (extrinsic feedback) methodologies, but self-worth seems primarily attained through actually being appreciated and accepted for who they are now by parents and other adult persons of influence, and just as they might become. It is intrinsic.

RECEIVED MAR 1 6 2015